The Developing Child

Recent decades have witnessed unprecedented advances in research on human development. In those same decades there have been profound changes in public policy toward children. Each book in the Developing Child series reflects the importance of such research in its own right and as it bears on the formulation of policy. It is the purpose of the series to make the findings of this research available to those who are responsible for raising a new generation and for shaping policy in its behalf. We hope that these books will provide rich and useful information for parents, educators, child-care professionals, students of developmental psychology, and all others concerned with the challenge of human growth.

Jerome Bruner
New York University
Michael Cole
University of California, San Diego
Barbara Lloyd
University of Sussex
SERIES EDITORS

The Developing Child Series

Schooling

Sylvia Farnham-Diggory

Harvard University Press
Cambridge, Massachusetts
London, England   1990

Copyright © 1990 by the President and Fellows of Harvard College
All rights reserved
Printed in the United States of America
10 9 8 7 6 5 4 3 2 1

This book is printed on acid-free paper, and its binding materials have
been chosen for strength and durability.

Library of Congress Cataloging-in-Publication Data

Farnham-Diggory, Sylvia.
  Schooling / Sylvia Farnham-Diggory.
    p.   cm.—(The Developing child)
  Includes bibliographical references.
  ISBN 0–674–79271–8 (alk. paper). — ISBN 0–674–79272–6 (pbk. : alk.
  paper)
  1. Cognitive learning—United States.   2. Curriculum change—United
States.   I. Title.   II. Series.
LB1060.F36   1990
370.11—dc20   89-37081
                                                                        CIP

Acknowledgments

This book owes a great deal to my colleagues in the College of Education at the University of Delaware, especially those in the Academic Studies Assistance Program (ASAP), who have worked with me to develop methods and materials to aid learning in students of all ages. I think first of my cherished friend Bob Hampel, who tirelessly read and reread versions of the manuscript and provided invaluable editorial guidance. David Johns, Assistant Director of ASAP, spent many hours helping me think through ideas; he also filled in for me administratively so I could keep writing.

Among the other colleagues who helped me forge my views, I would like to thank especially Marilynn Carver-Magnani, who developed the Intensive Literacy reading program described in Chapter 6; Michael Bend, who designed the computer-based components of the same program, described in Chapter 5; Patricia Howe, coordinator of our adult literacy program; the excellent teachers in our after-school reading programs, especially Marilyn Gwaltney, Barbara McQueen, Pat Moeller, and Priscilla Wriston; Mary Norton, who traveled to Scotland with me to investigate the Jordanhill materials described in Chapter 4; Chris Madden, our school psychologist, who helped me become aware of problems described in Chapter 7; Mark Grabowski, our fearless programmer, who joined our research team seven years ago, and who has somehow managed to put up with me ever since.

I also thank colleagues at Jordanhill College of Education in Glasgow, in particular, Robin Frame, Fred Rendell, and Patricia Watterson; Jearnine Wagner, Cindy Herbert, Susie Monday, Julia Jarrell, Susan Russell and other members of the Learning About Learning group that produced the Neighborhood Explorer program described in Chapter 4 and that greatly influenced my views of schooling (they will recognize their ideas on every page); Rodney Grant, seventh-grade teacher at Stornoway Primary School in the Hebrides, whose jubilant "Kings and Things" is described in Chapter 4; Philip Brown, formerly Head Teacher of Macdiarmid School on Skye, now teaching in Australia, whose Skye Plantation science program is described in Chapter 5; Captain Robbie Sutherland, now retired, who designed and managed the Nautical Studies program at Stromness Academy, Orkney, described in Chapter 5; Debbie Smith, whose Shadows curriculum is described in Chapter 5, and whose work can now be observed at West Park Elementary School in Newark, Delaware; Barbara White of the University of California at Berkeley, whose physics curriculum is described in Chapter 5; Betsy Granda and others from the Newark Center for Creative Learning, founded some twenty years ago and still managed by the same group of teachers (not many alternative schools can make that claim, a testimony to the strength of their philosophy), described in Chapter 8; Marlene James, Principal of Brookside School in Newark, Delaware, a remarkable school leader and community coordinator, a bit of whose philosophy is described in Chapter 8; and above all Allan Collins, of Bolt, Beranek and Newman in Cambridge, Massachusetts, and Northwestern University, who, with John Seely Brown and others, saw how the principles of cognitive science could be synthesized into the new educational paradigm of cognitive apprenticeship.

I am also grateful to Dean Frank Murray and former Provost Leon Campbell, who have provided a wonderfully supportive environment for the development of the ideas in this book. And I especially want to express deep gratitude to Kathy Murphy, Bette Perna, and Ruth Smith, whose cheerfulness, patience, and fiendish efficiency hold together a multitude of enterprises. *Schooling* could not even have been imagined, much less finished, without them.

I would further like to thank Harvard University Press, especially Arthur Rosenthal, the Director, who set me on course to write this book some years ago; Angela von der Lippe, Editor for the Behavioral Sciences, who steered me wisely and unswervingly through rough waters and smooth; and Elizabeth Gretz, my attentive manuscript editor.

And finally, I would like to thank, as I have so many times in the past, Jerry Bruner, whose visionary ideas, beginning in 1960 with the publication of *The Process of Education*, have guided my perceptions and growth, only one facet of which has been the writing of *Schooling*.

Contents

The Developing Child

Schooling

Introduction

This book is written for parents, teachers, college and graduate students, school administrators, civic leaders, corporate leaders, union leaders, and all other citizens who are concerned about the nature of contemporary schooling and its impact on children. My thesis is straightforward: your concerns are warranted. Contemporary schooling does not adequately prepare children for the adult world, and must be changed—but not necessarily in the directions indicated by reform efforts of the 1980s.

Concerns over the quality of contemporary education were starkly expressed in *A Nation at Risk*, published in 1983 by the National Commission on Excellence in Education. In a statement now famous, this report concluded: "The educational foundations of our society are presently being eroded by a rising tide of mediocrity that threatens our very future as a nation and as a people . . . If an unfriendly foreign power had attempted to impose on America the mediocre educational performance that exists today, we might well have viewed it as an act of war."[1]

Since 1983 reports on education in this country have cited relentlessly grim data. For example, only 4.9 percent of seventeen-year-olds read well enough to understand college-level textbooks.[2] On an international test of mathematical abilities, the great majority of United States children scored in the bottom 25 percent in comparison with other industrialized countries.[3] Scholastic Aptitude Test scores fell 68 points from 1967 to 1981, gained back 16 points by 1985, leveled off, and then dropped again in 1988.[4] Corporations must spend billions of dollars to remedy the basic education deficiencies of their employees; New York City alone is estimated to spend $1.5 billion annually on this problem.[5] Of even greater concern than deficiencies in the basic skills of reading, writing, and arithmetic are deficiencies in the higher-order skills of problem solving and decision making. As James Hunt comments, "it is in imparting the skills of analysis and problem-solving that constitute 'learning-to-learn' skills that our schools face their greatest need for improvement . . . The stiffening demands of advancing technology will . . . mean that real opportunity, real chances for upward mobility, will increasingly be reserved for those with 'learning-to-learn' skills: not just the ability to read, write, and compute at a minimal level, but more complex skills of problem solving, reasoning, conceptualizing, and analyzing. Increasingly, people who have only today's [1983's] basic skills—or less than today's basics—will be consigned to economic stagnation."[6]

The reasons that schoolchildren are failing to develop higher-order learning and thinking skills can be found in almost any classroom. One astute observer, John Goodlad, has described what he saw as follows:

> Students listened; they responded when called on to do so; they read short sections of textbooks; they wrote short responses to questions or chose from among alternatives in quizzes. But they rarely planned or initiated anything, read or wrote anything of some length,

or created their own products. And they scarcely ever speculated on meaning, discussed alternative interpretations, or engaged in projects calling for collaborative effort. Most of the time they listened or worked alone. The topics of the curriculum . . . were something to be acquired, not something to be explored, reckoned with, and converted into personal meaning and development.[7]

Even "good" students, children who do well in the type of classroom Goodlad describes, not only fail to acquire higher-order learning and thinking skills, but must actively learn to repress them.

Children in most of our schools can be thought of as trainees in a long-standing bureaucratic structure. Their primary job is to learn the role of "the pupil." Harry Gracey, after studying a middle-class suburban school, wrote a poignant description of the children he observed. About 35 percent of them, he said, identified with the pupil role; about 60 percent submitted to but did not identify with it; and 5 percent rebelled against it.

> Children who identify with the pupil role are those we have seen actively and enthusiastically participating in classroom activities. These children not only conform to the classroom norms, but attempt to excel in their terms, and as a consequence they become "good pupils." Being a good pupil becomes an important component of their developing self-images. There are almost always more girls than boys in this category . . .
>
> [However] the majority of children in any classroom seem to comply with the teacher's requirements without the enthusiasm of those who identify with the pupil role . . . These children will be the "average pupils" in that they will be "on grade level" in their achievement. They will comply with the requirements, but have no drive to put in an excellent performance . . . The school day [has become] a long, tedious ordeal . . .

> Children in rebellion against the pupil role, either pas-
> sively or actively, are usually referred to the school psy-
> chologist for testing . . . They generally test low in
> intelligence and ability, but this should be seen as part
> of their role rejection. They don't do well in class and
> they don't do well on out-of-class aptitude tests; they
> are rejecting the entire school organization and all its
> parts.[8]

Gracey was studying a school of the type that educa-
tion-conscious families often seek. Inner-city schools,
and schools in poor neighborhoods, would have many
more rebels and probably very few students who identified with the pupil role. Gracey makes clear that even in
what appears to be an ideal traditional school environment, children may succeed only at tremendous cost to
their own personal and intellectual development.

At best, the school reform efforts of the 1980s may
produce a few more "good pupil bureaucrats." The
types of reforms that have been imposed (often by state
law)—longer school hours, stricter promotion requirements, and so on—make it even more difficult for
schools to teach the problem-solving, reasoning, con-
ceptualizing, and analyzing skills that enable citizens to
escape from passive bureaucratic roles. School reform
typically means reassertion of traditional educational
structures and reorchestration of the traditional roles
that participants are expected to play. To quote Albert
Shanker, president of the American Federation of
Teachers: "Public education today is pretty much what
it was 50 or 100 years ago and . . . the usual idea of
educational reform is to go back to where we were in the
1930's. Nobody seems to be talking about restructuring
to do things differently."[9]

This book is about restructuring to do things differently.

*　　*　　*

Contemporary practice in our schools is based on a science of learning that has been superseded. Over the past three decades, we have discovered a great deal about how children work, learn, and grow. Schooling based on this new knowledge will look quite different from traditional schooling. Chapters 1 and 2 discuss these foundations, and Chapter 3 describes a new approach to education called "cognitive apprenticeship."

The next three chapters present curriculum samples that illustrate cognitive apprenticeship principles. The fundamental point is that instruction should begin with comprehensive, important, long-range projects within which basic skills training is embedded. This approach is diametrically opposed to the path of most traditional education, where basic skills are taught first, in more or less isolated ways, before a child is thought to have the foundation for more complex learning enterprises. In fact, our minds work the other way around. We are born into complex, interesting learning environments. We immediately start trying to figure out the "big picture." It is within this framework that we begin to master subskills like walking and talking. It is not the case that we learn the subskills first, and then put them together into an understanding of life.

Similarly, schooling should begin by establishing higher-order frameworks within which subskills like reading, writing, and calculating can function in organized and meaningful ways. It should be clear to the child why basic skills are important, and what they will empower the child to achieve. Chapter 4 thus describes several curriculums that fulfill one of the most important functions of schooling: preserving and transmitting the culture. Chapter 5 describes some equally large-scale approaches to science and technology. Chapter 6 then takes up the three R's. It presents principles that should govern the design of basic skills training programs and discusses ways to embed such programs in the overall curriculum.

The final chapters deal with mechanisms of change. Chapter 7 focuses on three key problems—the fractionated curriculum, classes that are formed by administrative edict rather than on the basis of interest, and instructional objectives that are defined in terms of paper-and-pencil tests—and suggests ways of mitigating their effects when it is not possible to escape them. Chapter 8, in contrast, discusses ways to escape them, and provides guidelines for pursuing three available options: working within the public system, starting an alternative school, or educating children at home. In the Conclusion I also briefly consider some special opportunities open to school-business partnerships.

My goal throughout has been to help relieve the frustration felt by teachers, parents, school administrators, and other concerned citizens—not to mention schoolchildren themselves—who want to make changes in our educational system, but don't know exactly what, how, or why. I have tried to provide concrete guidelines and, further, to explain where the guidelines have come from theoretically. Many alternate guidelines could be generated from the same set of theoretical principles, and I hope they will be.

The book has a positive cast. I don't say much about obstacles, for three reasons. One is that there are signs that the time has come for the educational changes described in this book, and that many projected obstacles will not materialize.[10] The second reason is that good teachers already know how to make these changes, and could begin making them immediately in every school in the country if they were empowered to do so. The third reason is that I really want us to get on with it, to get out of our armchairs and get to work. Ways of overcoming obstacles can always be found when citizens of good will are determined to find them.

Educating children is the most important enterprise we have. It is far more crucial than any so-called defense priority. It is our only true defense. We are talking about preparing the young of our species to make decisions about war and peace, to discover cures for AIDS, to solve problems of poverty and unemployment, overpopulation, world hunger, and the deadly leak of ozone through the holes in our atmosphere. The human population of this planet will survive only if today's adults begin now to design and support a new type of schooling, one that prepares tomorrow's adults to deal with the problems that are really there.

1 / Where Our Schools Are Coming From

There are two major approaches to the design of school programs. One begins with the child, the other, with the system.[1] The first is traceable to John Dewey and, before him, to Jean-Jacques Rousseau, and the second is traceable to Edward L. Thorndike; schools today reflect both positions. A child's developmental level, for example, determines grade placement, and the teaching materials used in each grade have been selected for children of a particular age. But the materials have been designed *for* children, not *by* children. The curriculum represents a fixed system through which children are passed. The curriculum does not grow from the needs and interests of a particular group of children in a particular classroom. Indeed, the very thought of developing such a curriculum may be startling. How could a school possibly invent a new curriculum for each group? How could standards be maintained? How could children be expected to know what they ought to learn?

Nevertheless, say Rousseau, Dewey, and their followers, true education cannot take place in any other way.

THE CHILD-CENTERED APPROACH

"Teach the child what is of use to a child and you will find that it takes all his time. Why urge him to studies of an age he may never reach, to the neglect of those studies which meet his present needs? 'But,' you ask, 'will it not be too late to learn what he ought to know when the time comes to use it?' I cannot tell; but this I do know, it is impossible to teach it sooner."[2] The author of these words, the famous philosopher, author, and social reformer, Jean-Jacques Rousseau, was born in Geneva in 1712 and died in 1778. He lived a wildly dramatic life: "Brilliant, erratic, and suspicious of rational ideas, Rousseau exhibited two personalities: a genius, first and foremost, with a remarkable intellect, he had an extraordinary talent developed with little formal education; at the same time, he was unstable, sensitive, devoid of emotional maturity, uprooted and alienated from the stabilizing influence of all social institutions."[3]

Despite this instability, or perhaps because of it, Rousseau formulated a grand plan for a good society. Believing that humans are inherently good but become corrupted by civilization, he preached essentially a return to a state of nature. Such arguments, passionately presented, captured the imagination. His radical political ideology played a part in the French Revolution and has been a continuing source of inspiration and provocation. In art and literature, his ideas have also had a profound effect. In education, his influence has been powerful beyond measure.

To present his educational views, Rousseau wrote *Emile*, a cross between a novel and a philosophical treatise. Emile was a boy being raised by his tutor, through whom Rousseau set forth the surprising notion that education should nurture a child's natural capabilities. Education, said Rousseau, should begin not where some adult has decided is appropriate, but where the child begins. Consider geography:

> In any study whatsoever, the symbols are of no value without the idea of the things symbolized. Yet the education of the child is confined to those symbols, while no one ever succeeds in making him understand the thing signified. You think you are teaching him what the world is like; he is only learning the map. He is taught the names of towns, countries, rivers, which have no existence for him except on the paper before him . . . After two years' work with the globe and cosmography, there is not a single ten-year-old child who could find his way . . . by a map about the paths of his father's estate without getting lost.
>
> [Emile's] geography will begin with the town he lives in and his father's country house, then the places between them, the rivers near them, and then the sun's aspect and how to find one's way by its aid . . . Let him make his own map, a very simple map, at first containing only two places; others may be added from time to time, as he is able to estimate their distance and position. You see at once what a good start we have given him by making his eyes his compass.[4]

Teach the child what is of use to a child, Rousseau kept emphasizing, and this is still a radical notion. Although some attempt is now made to teach through characters and events that are familiar to children, this device is still used in the service of ideas and principles that are essentially meaningless to the young. Many social studies curriculums, for example, introduce the postman and the fireman. But children are not really participants in the civic systems these characters symbolize. What are children participants in? Their own neighborhood playgroups and culture. Do such groups embody rules, customs, economic principles, laws, helping systems, communication strategies, and other matters of civic import? Of course they do, but few teachers or schools have constructed a social studies curriculum from the real-life experiences and problems that children must cope with on a daily basis. Instead, they use a curriculum that has been designed by a commercial publisher to appeal to as many textbook selection committees as possible. Children may find the curriculum interesting, but it is of very little use to them because it is quite remote from their world.

Development plays a much larger role in schooling today than it used to, however, thanks to Rousseau. Early schools were grim and punitive places. The first primers and spellers contained proverbs and Scripture selections. There was no thought of using materials that would be naturally interesting to children. There was no real concept of what a child was: children were simply deficient adults.[5] They were believed to lack knowledge, self-discipline, and any proper purpose, all of which had to be instilled, often painfully. With Rousseau, such ideas began to change.

In the early 1880s Johann Heinrich Pestalozzi, a disciple of Rousseau, established a school that embodied the educational principles expressed in *Emile*. It was visited by many Americans, and a Pestalozzi school was opened in Philadelphia in 1809. Another disciple, Friedrich Froebel, known as the father of kindergartens, opened a school in Frankfurt in 1816 and, about ten years later, published an influential book that described childhood as a divinely inspired and guided state. A follower of Froebel's, Mrs. Carl Shurz, opened the first American kindergarten, in Watertown, Wisconsin, in 1885. Fifteen years later there were over 4,500 kindergartens ("gardens where children grow") in the United States.

Also about 1900, William Torrey Harris, an innovative administrator who was also a philosopher (he founded the *Journal of Speculative Philosophy* and led what became known as the St. Louis philosophical movement), invented the K–8–4 schooling plan—one year of kindergarten, eight years of elementary school, and four years of secondary school. Subject matter and methods of instruction were to be adapted to suit the child's development during each period. Harris became the U.S. Commissioner of Education, a position that enabled him to spread his ideas widely.

Yet another educational leader with both administrative and philosophical gifts was Francis Parker, who was the founder of what became known as progressive education. In travels in Europe during the 1870s, he observed schools based on the ideas of Pestalozzi and Froebel. Froebel's work, in particular, inspired him. Parker's first opportunity to put his own educational ideas into practice came in Quincy, Massachusetts, where he served as the new superintendent of its failing school system. With great zeal, he threw out the traditional curriculum and replaced it with educational projects and experiences that were meaningful to children. Students learned geography by making clay models of mountains and rivers, for example, and their reading materials were keyed to such projects. This program, eventually referred to as the Quincy Plan, attracted national attention—especially after the Quincy children achieved higher scores than those received by other Massachusetts schoolchildren on state examinations.

In 1884 Parker brought his ideas to Cook County Normal School in Chicago, where he remained as principal for eighteen years. Concentrating on the theories of Rousseau, Pestalozzi, and Froebel, the school trained teachers and served as the public school for the surrounding neighborhood.[6]

The Dewey model. The spirit of child-centered education was carried forward by John Dewey, one of the world's greatest educational philosophers. Dewey was born in 1859 and grew up in Burlington, Vermont. He earned his doctorate at Johns Hopkins University, where he studied the theories of G. Stanley Hall, the founder of developmental psychology, and William James. Like so many others, Dewey said that James profoundly influenced his intellectual development. Another influence was William Torrey Harris, who accepted several of Dewey's first articles for the *Journal of Speculative Philosophy.*[7]

Dewey's philosophical quest was integrative. He searched for unities in ideas and experiences. In his view philosophy was not merely an abstract body of principles but also a guide to action in the world.[8] Believing that the purpose of effective thinking was to enrich human experience, he argued against compartmentalizing knowledge and experience. Dewey was also strongly influenced by theories of evolution and human development. He believed that thought and experience had emerged from earlier forms, and he therefore sought to explain the conditions that gave rise to human thinking and the natural evolution of thought. His ideas about integration and growth were central to the educational model he developed.

In 1894 Dewey became head of the departments of philosophy, psychology, and pedagogy at the University of Chicago, where he remained for ten years. During that period he founded a laboratory school—a concrete embodiment of his philosophy. The school opened in 1896 with 16 children and 2 teachers. Six years later it had 140 pupils ranging in age from four to fifteen, twenty-three teachers, and a host of university student assistants. Dewey left Chicago for Columbia University in 1904. He continued to write about education, but never again ran a school of his own. The eight short years of the Dewey laboratory school, however, gave great impetus to the progressive education movement, which became increasingly popular in the 1920s.

Three overarching principles guided the curriculum of the Dewey school: (1) instruction must focus on the development of the student's mind, not on blocks of subject matter; (2) instruction must be integrated and project-oriented, not divided into small units (for example, forty minutes of English, forty minutes of social studies); and (3) through the years of schooling, the progression of the curriculum must be from practical experiences (such as planting a garden) to formal subjects (such as botany) to integrated studies (such as the place of botany in the natural sciences).

To achieve these objectives, the Dewey curriculum was oriented around *occupations*—gardening, cooking, work with textiles, carpentry, hunting, mining, farming, trading, manufacturing, exploring unknown territories, producing artistic works, and scholarly research.

The study of occupations, Dewey said, permits children to learn in ways that are natural and interesting to them. Occupations always involve doing something; they engage and develop the child's motor skills and "hands-on" modes of learning. Occupations always involve making observations, analyzing, investigating, quantifying, and making predictions (as in baking a cake, for instance); they thus develop the child's scientific abilities. Occupations always involve other people; they encourage the child's social skills and interests. And occupations always require the exchange of ideas;

they thereby provide opportunities for training in communication.

In addition, Dewey's curriculum recapitulated the growth of the culture. Students began, as the culture had, with home and family, then took up trading and exploring, and finally ended with the formal academic disciplines (such as sociology) that the culture itself had developed after civilization had been established.

The daily procedures of the Dewey school have been described with care and charm by two sisters who taught in it—Katherine Camp Mayhew and Anna Camp Edwards.[9] If, with the aid of the recollections in their book, we visit the Dewey school on a day in 1905, we find a large, multiroomed house, in which groups of ten to twelve children of about the same age work together under the supervision of their teachers.

The kindergarten is in the living room of the house. It has banks of windows facing east, receiving the morning sun, a large fireplace, bookshelves, and several exits to the porch and gardens. The first principle of the kindergarten curriculum is that "no activity should be originated by imitation. The start must come from the child through suggestion; help may then be supplied in order to assist him to realize more definitely what it is he wants."[10]

The young children often suggest taking a walk in the nearby woods. On this day, we join their walk. As the children chatter excitedly about what they see, the teacher draws their attention to a bird's nest, a squirrel hole, and a rabbit hole. Talk turns to the subject of homes in general. The children realize they have homes, too. Where do homes come from? How does a bird build its nest? The children decide to pursue the question of where their own homes come from.

Houses are built of wood and brick, the children recognize, and building them requires tools. Visits to a lumber mill, a brickyard, and a hardware store are arranged. Naturally, the children decide to build a house of their own, as their teachers recount:

> Large boxes are used. The older children measured and cut all the paper for the walls. The little children tacked down the matting on the floors, made a table for the dining-room by fastening legs on a block. For chairs, they nailed a back to a cube and tacked on a leather seat. The older children made tables and chairs from uncut wood, which they measured and sawed by themselves [under close supervision, of course, often by fathers]. When finished, these were shellacked and the seats upholstered with leatherette and cotton. Some of the children painted the outside of the house so that its walls should be "protected from the weather." Inside it was papered "for ornament," and the necessary furniture for each room decided upon, made from cardboard, wood, or tin, and put into place. One of the results of this phase of the project was a gain in each child's ability to carry out his own ideas. He was put to it to execute and to show individual results. He thus secured the feel of accomplishment.[11]

The project fulfills the criteria that Dewey emphasized: hands-on activities; the scientific activities of observing, analyzing, investigating, quantifying, and making predictions; social cooperation; and exchange of ideas. The children also dictate reports of their activities, make up stories about imaginary families who live in their house, and compose letters about their house to send to friends and relatives. A teacher writes all this down, and the children are thus provided with written records that some of them can even begin to read.

The six-year-olds are headquartered in a room with large windows, alcoves, and nooks containing many plants and animals collected by the children. At the beginning of the day, the group makes plans and distributes jobs. Each child takes a turn as group leader. The day's written program is pinned to that child, so everyone can see at a glance what it is.

> The study of occupations as carried on during the year [in this age group] involved observation of seeds and their growth, or plants, wood, oil, stones, and animals . . . of geographical conditions of landscape, climate, and arrangement of land and water . . . No separation was made between the social side of the work, its concern with people's activities and their mutual dependencies, and the scientific side, its regard for physical facts and forces. Such conscious distinction between man and nature is the result of later reflection and abstraction.[12]

At the time of our visit, the children are engaged in the study of seeds and related occupations. They have been collecting seeds from the fields and the woods, and they have talked a great deal about how seeds are distributed—by wind, people, and animals. Each child has made lists of seeds and developed ways of classifying them. Seeds might be organized, for example, according to whether the "seed house" is good to eat, is not good to eat, or whether both seed and seed house are good to eat. Visits have been made to markets and farms, pictures have been collected and painted, and reports dictated and shared. The children have decided to plant a crop of winter wheat and are preparing a plot (five by ten feet) in the school yard. Questions of soil preparation have been addressed and resolved, the plot has been measured and marked, and the children are "plowing" with sharp sticks. They will shortly conclude that additional tools are called for, and the next several hours will be spent investigating and selecting better ones. When the wheat has grown, the children will thresh it, refine it, and bake a cake with it.

The seven-year-olds are engaged in the study of primitive life. Over the course of a year, they will investigate and re-create for themselves, in various models and re-enactments, as many aspects of early existence as possible: discovering fire and the problems in keeping fires going; cooking, by roasting and boiling with heated stones; gathering berries, roots, and fruits; trapping; inventing and finding materials for weapons for hunting (spears, axes, bows, and arrows); coordinating and leading hunts; migrating to follow grazing animals; soaking and drying animal sinews; making clay vessels; making clothing out of animal hides; domesticating animals; setting up permanent homesites; tribal cooperation; division of labor within communities; weaving cloth; trading and bartering; navigating rivers; discovering metals and smelting techniques; and the invention of agriculture. The children thus move from the beginnings of mankind through the Bronze Age. At the end of the year, they will summarize what they had learned in stories and plays.

The eight-year-olds are tracing the continuing development of civilization through the trading and exploration of the Phoenicians. The Phoenicians were selected in part because they served as a link between primitive societies and world travelers like Columbus. Through the Phoenicians, the children address the problem of what a tribe can do when it has no means of sustaining itself from the land alone. Go to sea and trade, the children decide. The Phoenicians are also important for their work in the sciences of geography, navigation, and physics. The children themselves confront the problems that gave rise to these disciplines: How do you plot a route? How do you decide how much weight a boat can carry? The solutions to these questions rely on the development of writing and mathematics, another significant reason to study this civilization.

> To carry on their work successfully the first merchant and trader would need . . . a system of measurements and weights. He would need a numerical system and a system of records . . .
>
> The question of records seemed easiest and the child who acted as trader at the time devised his own system of records. This was usually a picture of the article exchanged with marks by each to indicate the number exchanged.
>
> . . . At this moment of partial solution of their immediate problem as traders, namely, that of developing a practical method of barter, the children's interest was easily directed to the standards and tables of measurement used today . . . The children were shown primitive systems of counting [and invented additional systems of their own].
>
> . . . Concurrent with the construction of the number system, the need for a more accurate method of written record than that of rude pictures was felt . . . A sign to stand for a sound resulting in an alphabet was worked out . . . The arbitrariness of this system was reflected in two alphabets invented by the children. All this gave meaning to the reading and writing which were emphasized in this year.[13]

At the secondary level, the thirteen-year-olds have moved through the study of comparative civilizations. They have begun to abstract the principles that underlie their concrete experiences. They have studied life in an English village and compared it with life in a colonial American village. They have examined the significance of a point of view—looking at the feudal system from the contrasting perspectives of landowners and serfs. Mathematics and science have also been examined comparatively. The children have learned the metric system, and they have compared early French inventions with early American ones.

By this age, the youngsters are beginning to study formal disciplines, such as psychology, sociology, and physics, as systems of ideas that are independent of the people and social conditions that initially gave rise to them. Methods of formal research, in contrast to informal field experiences, are now a major focus in class.

There is emphasis upon reflection and personal synthesis. The pupils are encouraged to formulate and express a philosophy of learning.

> These children of the present followed the fast moving life-stream of the past. Through the power of imaginative thinking, each child became . . . one of its currents and was swept into and carried on to a more sympathetic understanding of the dynamic story of the race. Little by little the idea was born that the use of thinking is to manage experience. This idea . . . grew into a consciously formulated principle . . . Each child began to see the value of reviews, of summaries, of the analysis of a problem or a situation, of the classification of facts into their categories, and the logical arrangement of knowledge to facilitate its further use in any field of activity.[14]

In pursuing these objectives, it can be important to construct alternative ways of presenting information. The practical study of photography, for example, is an opportunity to learn about the abstract principles governing light, optics, and perspective.

In keeping with the changing social interests of adolescents, clubs are springing up. There is a Camera Club and, of course, a Dewey Club for philosophical discussion and debate. But connections with practicality are never lost. Putting their highly practiced construction skills to work, the youngsters build themselves a club-house.

The success of such a curriculum depended greatly upon the creativity and organizational skills of teachers. Little could be specified in advance: the very point of the Dewey curriculum was that it grow from the natural capacities and experiences of the children involved, not from the head of an academician.

> The child is the starting-point, the center, and the end. His development, his growth, is the ideal. It alone furnishes the standard . . . Personality, character, is more than subject-matter. Not knowledge or information, but self-realization is the goal. To possess all the world of knowledge and lose one's own self is as awful a fate in education as in religion. Moreover, subject-matter never can be got into the child from without. Learning is active. It involves reaching out of the mind. It involves organic assimilation starting from within. Literally, we must take our stand with the child and our departure from him.[15]

In theory, this ideal is unassailable. In practice, it has proved largely unattainable. We simply do not know how to train large numbers of teachers to create spontaneous learning environments in collaboration with children. It has proved much easier to train teachers and administrators in the systems approach.

THE SYSTEMS APPROACH

In 1910 in Gary, Indiana, William A. Wirt, an enterprising school superintendent inspired by the new models of factory efficiency, invented what was then called the *platoon school*.

The plan was arranged so that all of the rooms, either home rooms or special rooms, were in constant use. For example, while one group was in its home room receiving instruction in reading, writing, and arithmetic, another group was in the music room, another in the shop, another on the playground, etc. When the bell rang, the students would shift to the next class . . . obviously to function effectively this scheme required a high degree of administrative planning and precision timing in the moving of children. This was particularly true if the schools were large, as they were at Gary, when some of them included all 12 grades and eventually had as many as 3000 students.[16]

Wirt believed he was fostering a child-centered plan. He called his plan the "work-study-play" system, since students, when not in their academic classes, received training in many real-life activities that appeared to center upon children and their needs. The educational program did not grow from the children, however, as Dewey's program did. Knowledge was attached to children, somewhat as the parts of an automobile—bumper, headlights, and so on—are attached to basic frames. The same efficiency concepts that led to the development of the assembly line, in fact, were at the heart of the platoon school movement.[17]

As educators in the early 1900s began to run schools like factories, many aspects of schooling that we take for granted today were transferred directly from machine shops to classrooms. There are now standardized ways of keeping records, planning curriculums, furnishing classrooms, dividing up school days (into periods), dividing up curriculum (into units and lessons), administering discipline, instructing, and grading. Every school, every district, and every state has manuals that detail exactly how things are to be done. Ideas of quality control and interchangeability were borrowed from the workplace and applied to education.

At the same time that these changes were occurring in educational practice, a corollary movement, behaviorism, was developing within the then new science of psychology. Behaviorism emphasized the precise quantification of the conditions of learning (the input) and the learner's response (the output).

The Thorndike model. Edward L. Thorndike, born in 1874, was a leader in this new field of psychology, especially in its application to education. Like Dewey, he was strongly influenced by William James, with whom he studied at Harvard University, even keeping his experimental animals (chickens) in James's basement.[18] Thorndike finished his doctoral degree at Columbia University and spent the major part of his professional career at Teachers College, the Columbia University affiliate. Dewey too ended up at Columbia, but for reasons that will soon be clear, there are few records of encounters between them.

With John B. Watson, Pavlov, and other founders of behaviorism, Thorndike's objective was to transform psychology into a quantitative field. Anything that exists, Thorndike used to say, exists in some amount.[19] It follows that there is always a way to measure it. Once a measurement is made, it can be used to formulate scientific predictions.

In psychology, what can be measured is the stimulus, or the situation, as Thorndike preferred to call it, and the response. In the laboratory, the brightness of a signal light can be quantified. The speed of a subject's response to this stimulus—say, pressing a switch upon seeing the light—can also be quantified. Theories about the connections between them (the psychological equivalent of an equation) enable the researcher to predict changes in the response as a function of changes in the stimulus.

In the classroom, Thorndike said, items to be learned—such as vocabulary words or arithmetic facts— could be quantified, as could the speed and accuracy of a pupil's response. With a theory of the relationship between what goes into a student in the classroom and what comes out, Thorndike had a science of education.

Thorndike theorized that a stimulus and a response are related by a bond between them that comes into existence under certain conditions. He formulated these conditions as three main laws and five subsidiary principles:

The Laws
- *The law of exercise.* Repetition strengthens ("stamps in") bonds.
- *The law of effect.* Bonds followed by a "satisfying" state of affairs will be strengthened; bonds followed by an "annoying" (or boring) state will be weakened.
- *The law of readiness.* What "satisfies" or "annoys" will be determined, in part, by the student's inner state of preparedness or interest.

The Principles
- *Overall attitude and expectations guide learning.* General ideas that students bring to a task influence learning.
- *The learner is selective.* Bonds will form between only some of the available stimuli and responses. Students may or may not spontaneously select the ones that the teacher has in mind.
- *Trial and error is to be expected.* Students try out some wrong responses before discovering the correct ones.
- *Analog responses are to be expected.* Responses that resemble previously successful ones are likely to be tried again.
- *Responses gradually shift to new stimuli.* For generalization to occur, a new learning situation should initially resemble an old one, and gradually change.

These laws and principles are still highly visible in today's schools. Schools arrange for students to practice (the law of exercise); they grade them (the law of effect); they provide materials that suit a student's level of ability or age (the law of readiness); they urge parents to instill positive attitudes toward school; they try to guard against the fact the students can miss the point of instructional episodes; they expect initial trial and error with gradual improvement over time; they recognize that students may continue to apply a method that worked earlier; and they know that students will need special guidance in transferring old knowledge to new situations.

More striking is the continuing emphasis on Thorndike's preoccupation with counting, measuring, and predicting. All curriculum materials and instructional procedures today are broken up into countable units— ditto pages, workbook pages, daily lessons, fifty-minute periods, sets of exercises, and so on. One reason for this is that Thorndike introduced the practice now referred to as *task analysis*—identifying the components of a complex task so that each can be taught more or less separately. He analyzed the task of adding a column of numbers, for example, as involving:

> Learning to keep one's place in the column as [one] adds.
> Learning to keep in mind the result of each addition until the next number is added to it.
> Learning to add a seen to a thought-of number.
> Learning to neglect 0s in the columns.
> . . . Learning to "carry" [which] involves in itself at least two distinct processes.[20]

Thorndike believed that each of these processes was "psychologically distinct" and required "distinct educational treatment." It is clear that breaking down tasks in this manner facilitated measurement and control of the instructional program.

Testing was, predictably, Thorndike's favored method of measuring outcomes. He was fascinated by the challenge of devising ways to measure human traits, attitudes, abilities, skills, and knowledge. Counting correct answers was only the beginning: Thorndike developed scales for rating handwriting, English composition, and drawing. By the 1920s, hundreds of tests had been published by Teachers College, and schools throughout the country were using them. Thorndike's theory that testing was the only *scientific* way to measure achievement was widely accepted.

A particular advantage of tests is that they make it possible to specify instructional goals in terms that are easily quantifiable. Instead of saying, "The child is expected to learn . . . ," a teacher can say, "The child is expected to answer correctly eight out of ten questions on this test." These are today called *behavioral objectives*, and teachers are routinely trained to set them—that is, to conceptualize the goals they set for children's mental growth in terms of "percent correct on tests."

The seeds of almost every pedagogical technique can be traced to Thorndike's programs at Teachers College. There is, in fact, a direct line of transmission. By 1940, when Thorndike retired, nearly one teacher in ten in the United States had attended Teachers College. More than two out of every ten big-city school superintendents had been trained there, as had nearly three out of every ten deans of colleges of education. Instructional practice as we know it today preserves, in more sophisticated and elaborate forms, the fundamental principles that Edward Thorndike invented some seventy years ago.

THORNDIKE'S LEGACY

Although today's schools reflect the viewpoints of both Dewey and Thorndike, Thorndike has largely prevailed. His systems were highly compatible with those adopted by burgeoning educational bureaucracies and industries, while Dewey's philosophy was not. Thorndike's emphasis on quantitative measurement today characterizes almost every aspect of educational planning, performance, and evaluation. Legislators and state school boards explain allocations and policies in terms of scores on competency tests or time spent on particular subjects. Commercial test and textbook publishers generate billion-dollar businesses accordingly. Children's progress is precisely charted in terms of answers right and pages covered. Contemporary education is still largely driven by psychological principles similar to those Thorndike originated in a doctoral thesis over a century ago.

Thus, the schoolchild of the late twentieth century is but a very small cog in an enormously complex educational machine that continues to justify itself primarily in terms of early twentieth-century theoretical concepts. What can the child do other than learn to fit in, to become a proper bureaucrat? What else can schools do? To begin with, they can adopt a whole new scientific foundation, which is the subject of the next chapter.

2/ The Advent of Cognitive Science

In the 1950s, new paradigms began to replace behaviorism in basic psychological science. The paradigms were interdisciplinary; they incorporated ideas from philosophy, anthropology, neurology, linguistics, and especially from the new field of artificial intelligence, a branch of computer science. The interdisciplinary paradigms defined a field now called *cognitive science*.[1] It is from this field that contemporary educational designers should draw their guiding principles.

A fundamental tenet of cognitive science is that the study of complex phenomena like thinking and learning must be guided by adequately complex theoretical models. Many models are possible. Figure 1, for example, depicts two concept networks for numbers. The first network represents knowledge of a three-digit number symbol, 123. Its many components include knowledge of the right-to-left spatial relationships of the digits (d_1, d_2, and d_3), number names, place values, and knowledge that digits range from 0 to 9. The second network represents a different set of number concepts, derived from physical materials—concrete blocks or cubes. The concept network in this case includes knowledge of groups and subgroups. Numerical quantity is directly represented here, unlike in the first network, where it

Symbolic Representation
of Number
(1 2 3)

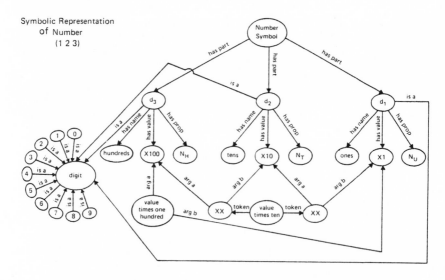

Physical Representation
of Number

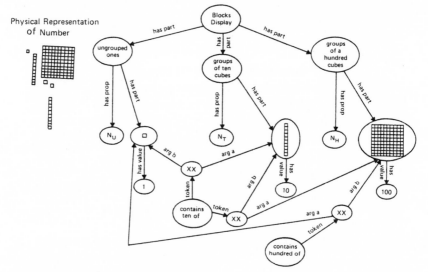

1. Two concept networks for numbers. *Top:* numbers as written symbols; *bottom:* numbers as concrete blocks.

must be inferred from the interaction between digit and place. Another difference is that in the first network, the location of an element matters; in the second, it does not.

The diagrams in Figure 1 were constructed by Audrey Champagne and her colleagues at the Learning Research and Development Center of the University of Pittsburgh to guide the design of a series of mathematics lessons.[2] The models represent a small portion of the expertise of a mathematically competent person— expertise that the lessons were designed to impart. A complete depiction of mathematical knowledge would, of course, be far more complicated. It would include knowledge of procedures (addition, subtraction), knowledge of the logic of the number system, knowledge of practical operations (such as making change and adding minutes), knowledge of classroom methods for teaching mathematics, knowledge of the kinds of problems that can be solved mathematically, knowledge of sources for getting help, and so on. Probably only a relatively small part of such knowledge can be verbalized. The larger part is tacit; it can be demonstrated, but it is difficult to describe in words. This fact has important implications for instruction, as we shall see in Chapter 3.

Since the 1950s an enormous amount of work has gone into the construction of models of human thinking and learning. Many of these models have been in the form of computer programs, which provide new and powerful theoretical languages.[3] Currently, for example, my research group at the University of Delaware is exploring neural network models of the severe reading disability known as dyslexia. We are simulating on the computer five different types of impairments that can produce reading errors, and comparing the output to that of dyslexic children. The impairments are extremely complex theoretically, involving—as reading must—the perception of words and pieces of words, knowledge of letter-sound correspondence rules in English, the processing of feedback, task persistence, and learning rates. New theoretical languages enable researchers to deal with the true complexity of the processes behind a child's production of even a single word on a reading test.[4]

THE ARCHITECTURE OF COGNITION

Cognitive scientists have borrowed from computer scientists the term *system architecture* to describe the general features of human thinking. These features are represented in Figure 2, with broken lines indicating that

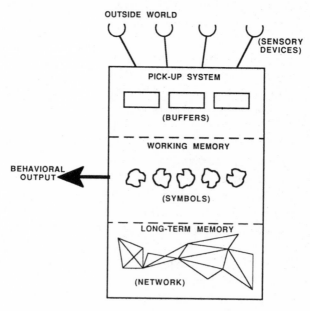

2. Architecture of the cognitive system.

the separation between the three main sections, or structures, is not sharp. All three structures interact extensively in complex ways.[5]

The pick-up system. The pick-up system is the part of the mind that takes in information from the outside world. It includes sensory devices (eyes, ears, hands) and very short-term sensory holding devices, or buffers. Information that comes in through the senses is maintained for brief periods in buffers. The raw image of a face seen in a flash of lightning, for example, will remain lit up in the mind's eye (the visual buffer) for about a quarter of a second. Auditory and tactual sensations are preserved for longer periods, sometimes up to four seconds, before they disappear.

Working memory. Working memory is the executive region of the mind. It organizes information that comes in from the outside world through the pick-up system as well as information that is already inside long-term memory. The organization is in the form of working-memory programs, which are goal-directed sequences of operations. These programs are the governing forces behind behavioral output (shown at the left of the figure).

The relationship between the pick-up system and working memory keeps the mind from being overwhelmed by sensory impressions. During the brief period when sensory information is being held in buffers, working memory decides whether the information is relevant to one of its programs. If so, it will bring the information into working memory by constructing a symbol for it. If you remember the face in that lightning flash for longer than a quarter of a second, it's because your working memory has constructed an image of it.

The raw sensory analog of the face has disappeared from your brain, but the experience has now been symbolized.

When sensory information is not useful, working memory ignores it. The buffers clear, and become ready for new impressions. Although you are continually scanning the world, your mind is not overwhelmed by sensations because you are not maintaining that sensory information in the form of symbols.

Theories of how working memory functions must explain a mystery. Working memory has a limited immediate work span, which means that it can deal with only a few items during any given instant. Yet somehow it maintains programmatic control of the contents of that work span—behavior remains organized from one instant to the next. How does this happen?

For the next minute, look at the scene in front of you and try to be conscious of everything in it at once. Try as you might, your attention will switch rapidly from one small set of items to another. You can't make yourself be aware of everything at once. Yet during that period, you didn't forget what you were doing. As your attention switched about, you remembered your objective, kept track of improvements or failures, came up with new strategies, and finally decided it was time to go back to reading. Your working memory compiled and ran a mental program that maintained continuity from one act of attending to the next.

A working-memory program comes into existence whenever a goal is set up. A mental plan for achieving that goal immediately begins to put itself together. Associated with a goal is knowledge about it—facts, concepts, skills, and so on. The goal primes that knowledge and also sensitizes an individual to particular sensory cues. If the goal is to open a door, the person becomes especially sensitive to doorknob, edge, and motion cues. As the working-memory plan unfolds, it triggers behavior—movement and speech. Working memory monitors its own operations, as well. It keeps track of progress and deletes the program when the goal has been achieved or abandoned.

Throughout the day, one goal after another assembles one program after another in our working memories. Goals are always active in the mind, and working memory organizes its operations accordingly, bringing order and continuity to human experience.

Long-term memory. The mind is in part a gigantic repository of information. In some remarkable fashion, the human brain maintains records of information it has processed—possibly all the information it has ever processed. These records constitute what cognitive psychologists call long-term memory.

Long-term memory has been described as associational in structure at least since Aristotle, who noted that minds "pass rapidly from one step to the next; for instance from milk to white, from white to air, from air to damp; after which one recollects autumn, supposing that one is trying to recollect that season."[6] Currently, long-term memory is described in terms of a network, a view that has been strongly influenced by work in artificial intelligence.

In a computer, information is stored at a particular address, called a node. The information can be linked to other information—another node—by a relation of some kind. For example, *Mary* can be linked to *John* on the basis of a love relation. *Mary* and *John* can also be linked to other nodes by other relations. We can diagram this as shown in Figure 3. The nodes are circles, and the relations are arrows linking the nodes. Note that the

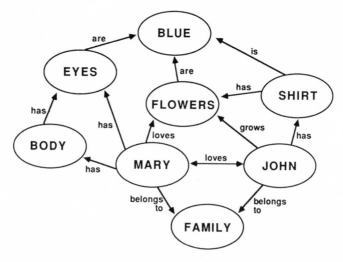

3. Fragment of a long-term memory network.

arrows are directional. *Mary* has *eyes*, for example; *eyes* don't have *Mary*.

Figure 3 is a fragment of a node-linked memory network—a set of addresses that are interconnected. To retrieve information from this type of computer network, a programmer says something like, "Go to the address *Mary* and print out everything linked to it." The computer then lists its "knowledge" about *Mary:*

Mary

has eyes

loves flowers

loves John

member of a family

If someone asked you to write down what you know about a particular individual, you might produce a similar list. Human memory can also be described as a network of nodes that are linked to other nodes by particular relations.

Knowledge is a set of linked nodes, a portion of a long-term memory network. When one node is activated, related nodes are primed. Having a lot of knowledge means that a portion of the long-term memory network is dense and that activation can spread quickly from one node to another.

Some knowledge clusters are qualitatively different from others, however. The cluster that makes up my knowledge of a dance step is quite different from the cluster that makes up my knowledge of the history of the ballet. At present, cognitive scientists are studying five types of knowledge that appear to be qualitatively distinct from one another. They can be distinguished in terms of their characteristics and also in terms of the way they are acquired.[7]

Declarative knowledge is knowledge of facts: that a dancer named Mikhail Baryshnikov defected from Russia on July 1, 1974, for example. These are facts I can "declare" to you in words. You, in turn, can declare those facts to someone else. Declarative knowledge is acquired through spoken or written words, for the most part, though it can also be acquired from mathematical notation, gestural language, or some other type of code. Most academic knowledge is of this type.

Procedural knowledge is skill knowledge, knowledge of how to do something. It is knowledge that has to be displayed, such as a dance step, and it is acquired by doing. Procedures are learned through practice. With sufficient practice, procedures become automatic; they run themselves, and deliberately thinking about them may even disrupt them.

Conceptual knowledge is knowledge of general forms or prototypes. It may be categorical in nature, such as knowledge of different types of dance costumes. It can also be schematic or scriptlike in nature, such as knowledge of dance movement diagrams or of the stories that classical ballets depict. I have constructed a concept of classical ballet from having seen many different examples of ballets. I have also read about them, so I have some declarative knowledge of classical ballet forms as well. But by definition, concepts are not acquired declaratively. Conceptual knowledge comes into existence inductively, through personal, repeated exposure to examples.

Analogical knowledge is knowledge that preserves the patterned structure of information, as a visual memory does. My knowledge of Baryshnikov's face is analogical. The pattern in my mind preserves the relationship of a particular nose to a particular set of eyes. That knowledge is qualitatively different from my concept of a male ballet star and from my knowledge of facts about Baryshnikov's career. Analogical knowledge can only come into existence through the activation of the senses; it is a collection of sensory memories.

Logical knowledge is a personal theory of how something works, an explanation, a way of accounting for a phenomenon. Logical knowledge can be formal for someone trained as a scientist, but much logical knowledge has an informal structure. I theorized that I like ballet because it so completely captures my attention that I stop thinking about other matters. Music or pictures alone do not do that for me, but when the two are combined, I am fully absorbed. This informal theory came into existence through my own reasoning, and I am satisfied with it; it accounts for something that I wanted to make sense of. Note that if an explanation is declared *to* you, it is declarative knowledge, by definition, not logical knowledge. Logical knowledge, whether it is true or not, comes into existence only through personal reasoning.

THE DEVELOPMENT OF COGNITION

The human information-processing system develops and grows; it does not start out fully formed. But humans are born with remarkable abilities. Over the past two decades, thanks in part to new technologies, there have been astounding discoveries about the capacities of children and babies. It has been shown, for example, that newborns can discriminate small variations in number, such as the difference between two taps and three taps. They can even distinguish two taps from three light blinks—which is to say that they are truly discriminating quantities, not merely sensations.[8] The development of these cognitive abilities can be examined within the framework of the adult architecture.

Development of the pick-up system. The ability to hear, see, smell, and feel is present at birth. Evolution has equipped the human infant with sensory anatomy that is "ready to go": the infant just has to stay awake long enough to find out it's there, and to begin learning to use it.[9]

Learning is aided by the fact that sensory memories in infants and young children last much longer than they do in older children and adults. If an infant sees a face in a flash of lightning, the image stays lit up in the mind's eye for as long as two seconds, eight times as long as for adults. Suppose you're just learning that the furry creature with four legs and a tail is called "kitty." When you see a cat, you have to get "kitty" out of your long-term memory and into your working memory. If you're new at searching your memory for names, that may take a while. The super-holding capacities of young buffers provides young working memories the extra time they need to deal with incoming information and construct symbols for it.

Development of working memory. The two main characteristics of the working memory, a limited span of apprehension (the work span) and programmatic capacity (goal setting, and so on), improve with development, in part because everything is becoming more familiar.

The work span has been traditionally measured by asking people to repeat back a random list of numbers that they have just listened to. At the age of two, a child will be able to repeat back about two numbers. By the age of seven, she will be up to five. The adult span is about seven. It used to be thought that this course of development was a sign of increasing capacity. But we now believe that capacity increases only up to a span of three or four items. Beyond that, improvements are attributable to familiarity.[10] Adults, unlike children, are highly practiced in remembering sequences of unrelated numbers—telephone numbers and zip codes, for example. If adults are presented with unfamiliar materials, such as a string of foreign words, the number they can recall drops back to three or four.

Working-memory programs change in two ways with development. They become more complex, and they operate more quickly. Table 1 lists tasks and questions used to test preschoolers of various ages. Their abilities illustrate the growing capacity to construct increasingly complex working-memory programs across a variety of domains. Sentences become longer and more complex, block structures become more elaborate and hierarchical—(small structures are put together into larger

Table 1 Examples of increasingly complex working-memory programs constructed by young children

Age (in years)	Imitating sentences	Block building	Following instuctions
1.0–1.9	Say: "Ball"; "Daddy"	(Place one block)	"Go get the ball."
2.0–2.9	Say: "I'm a big girl."	(Make line of blocks)	"Put the button in the box."
3.0–3.9	Say: "Jack likes to feed the little puppies."	(Make block pattern)	"Open the door; then bring the box to me."
4.0–5.9	Say: "Jack likes to feed the little puppies in the barn."	(More complex pattern)	"Put the pencil on the chair; open the door; bring the box to me."

Source: Robbie Case, "Intellectual Development from Birth to Adulthood: A Neo-Piagetian Interpretation," in Children's Thinking: What Develops? ed. R. S. Siegler (Hillsdale, N.J.: Erlbaum, 1978), table 2.4.

ones), and longer strings of instructional subroutines can be remembered and carried out.[11]

Such programs are not only more complex; they are also assembled and activated more quickly. It's as if all working-memory operations speed up with growth. Goals are set more rapidly, cues are noticed faster, and so on. The whole program runs more efficiently. Mental-processing rates of older children and adults are faster in every way than those of young children. This may be in part a matter of practice and experience and in part a matter of neurological maturation. The number of brain connections multiplies, and transmission rates increase.[12]

Development of long-term memory. The most dramatic changes as a child grows occur in the realm of knowledge. Every waking moment, children add to their stock of information. In language development alone, it is estimated that preschoolers learn about nine new words a day, one word for every waking hour. By the age of six they know 14,000 words, on the average.[13] Each of the five different types of knowledge develops at its own rate.

We would never think of trying to explain something to an infant in words. Not until a child is about a year old do verbal explanations begin to take hold, and the acquisition of declarative knowledge, therefore, probably doesn't begin much before that time. A younger child may recognize intonation patterns, but the patterns don't function as vehicles for transmitting facts.

Once declarative knowledge begins to accrue, there is an explosion of declarative-memory network construction, as the rate of vocabulary growth illustrates. This doesn't mean, however, that young children understand words or facts in the same way that older children and adults do. The words are not linked to the same kinds of information. In an adult memory, the word *blue* in Figure 3 would also be linked to objects other than Mary's eyes. In a young child's declarative memory, *blue* may be linked only to a particular object, such as a crayon.

Procedural knowledge is acquired rapidly and continuously from birth. Much of what young children know is procedural in form. Ask a young child how old she is, and she will hold up some fingers. Ask her where the dog is, and she will look toward the back door. Her knowledge is in the form of actions. Jerome Bruner has called this type of early knowledge *enactive*.[14] It is acquired in prodigious amounts throughout childhood. Generally, it is much easier for young children to show you what they know than to tell you.

Children can be shown to have acquired conceptual knowledge as early as we can measure it. By the age of nine months, infants, given an array of objects to play with, can sometimes be observed touching objects from a same category (blocks) in sequence, before touching objects from a different category (toy people).[15] Schematic knowledge can also be observed at an early age. After a few visits to different supermarkets, a young child will expect to be placed in a cart and will immediately start looking for familiar packages, demonstrating that she has formed a "supermarket schema" or "script." She has a general concept that incorporates setting, props, sequences of events, and roles. Of course she may not be right about everything. She probably thinks the cashier pays *you* when you leave.

Conceptual knowledge gradually becomes hierarchical. A child learns that supermarkets belong to a general class of stores, and that stores in turn belong to a higher-order class of commercial enterprises. Although young children may not yet have constructed that particular hierarchy, their more familiar concepts may be hierarchical in form. When researchers charted a four-year-old's knowledge of dinosaurs, they discovered that his concepts spontaneously fell into the same categories found in biology textbooks. He grouped dinosaurs into meat-eating and plant-eating categories, and so on. The conceptual structures of young children who "specialize" in some domain may be surprisingly sophisticated.[16]

Infants and preschoolers have truly remarkable capacities for storing analogical data. In another study, preschoolers were shown dozens of pictures of familiar objects—toys, food, and the like. Some of the pictures were shown only once, and others were shown again, in order to find out whether the children realized that they had seen certain pictures before. The children identified pictures they had seen before with 98 percent accuracy, even when the repeated pictures were separated by as many as twenty-five intervening pictures. After a week, the children still recognized pictures they had seen only once before with 75 percent accuracy.[17]

Analogical knowledge doesn't change with development, but it does get used more effectively. Young children may not realize that sensory memories can be aids to the recall of other information, such as facts or concepts.

Children are born with impressive logical capacities, which can be illustrated by an examination of their first words. Table 2 contains a sample of new words spoken by a little boy named Willis. His logical capacities are visible in the very first words in his vocabulary: *dog, ball, down,* and *hot*. In them he is expressing the notion that things can do things, that objects can act or be acted upon, or modified, and that they have locations. These fundamental logical ideas appear in the language of children all over the world.[18]

Table 2 Early words

Age of child (in months)	Child's word	True word	What was going on?
11	Daw	Dog	First repeated after being shown a picture; later generalized to pictures and real animal.
11	Ball	Ball	Balls have always been favorite toy—child said it on own.
11	Down (emphasis on *w*)	Down	Threw a toy off his changing table—said "down."
11	Hot	Hot	Parents always empha- sized "hot" when coffee mugs were on table—he suddenly started repeating.
11	Hi	Hi	Response to someone saying hi to him.
12	1. Mē-Mē 2. Mămē 3. Mommy	Mommy	Mother gets all three, depending on what mood child is in.
12	Eye	Eye	Parents play "name the parts" while changing him. One day child was holding his doll, pointed to the eye, and said the word.
13	Baby (sometimes bēbē)	Baby	Repeated after being shown picture in magazine.

There are other logical ideas buried in the items in the table, as well. Things can have names. Saying names can have effects on people. Words can accompany actions. Things can cause sensations—pain, falling, being picked up. Social conventions exist. Ideas and experiences can be represented by words, and new words for them can be requested. All these fundamental philosophical insights are displayed by an infant who has only been on the planet for a few hundred days.

With development, more elaborate personal theories are constructed. These were of special interest to the famous Swiss developmental theorist, Jean Piaget. Some of his earliest work concerned the development of moral theories in children.[19] Why is an action punishable? If a child breaks fifteen cups by accident, is that worse than breaking one cup on purpose? The young child's theory about this focuses on the magnitude of the disaster. By the age of ten, the child will take intention into consideration. By adulthood, our minds are stocked with multitudes of personal theories about events ranging from the weather to the causes of war.

IMPLICATIONS FOR EDUCATION

Emerging from contemporary research in cognition and development is a new picture of the mind. Humans come into the world with highly sophisticated mechanisms for acquiring knowledge. Spontaneously and continuously they construct programs for learning. These programs are headed by goals (actually hierarchies of goals and subgoals). The goals prime knowledge, enhance awareness of environmental cues, activate behavior, and respond to feedback. The almost miraculous rate at which young humans acquire whatever language(s) they are immersed in illustrates these inborn self-programming learning capabilities. By the time children reach the age of formal schooling, they have forged elaborate learning skills, and their minds are prodigiously complex repositories of knowledge. The feeling that a parent has, watching a young child grow, that "my child is brilliant, possibly even a genius," is entirely valid. Each child *is* extraordinary. Nature has equipped every child with learning capacities that far exceed anyone's ability to describe them.

Unfortunately, the formal educational system—based as it is on outdated, incorrect, oversimplified psychological principles—all too often collides catastrophically with children's natural learning skills, teaches them to mistrust and repress those skills, and moves countless numbers of children through 15,000 hours of systematic training in learning *not* to learn. All this occurs, moreover, while the brain is particularly receptive and adaptive—a special growth period that it has taken the human species millions of years to evolve.

From the first day of kindergarten, most children are taught that they should not set their own goals for learning or construct their own learning programs. Schools, they are taught, will do this for them. Schools will tell them when to turn their minds on, and when to turn them off, typically in twenty- to forty-minute cycles. Schools do not permit prolonged mental engagement in time-consuming, complex projects. Schools thus abdicate a fundamental responsibility: that of showing children how to improve the learning strategies they have already constructed for themselves. Children will learn spontaneously. What they need help in, from experts, is how to learn better—how to upgrade their own self-designed, perhaps environmentally restricted, working-memory programs for acquiring knowledge.

Unfortunately, many children are taught that the

knowledge they bring *to* school—including their knowledge of their own learning styles and capabilities—is at best a nuisance, since it upsets a program of instruction that has not been designed to address individual differences. Schoolchildren are typically also taught, year in and year out, to inhibit their awareness of environmental cues. They are trained to pay attention only to the very small set of cues emitted by the teacher, and to stop paying attention to almost everything else.

Many pupils must further learn that feedback—information about how personal learning programs should be adjusted—will not be delivered in time for it to be of any use. Feedback is usually in the form of grades, and grades are delivered so long after working-memory learning programs are active that the programs can scarcely be remembered, much less adjusted. And even then, what does a grade signify? What should the child adjust? Did he set the wrong goal? Did she respond to the wrong cue? Did he apply the wrong previous knowledge? Did she fail to process feedback?

Overall, from their first step into the classroom, most children discover that the rules that have governed their previous learning, and that continue to govern much of their out-of-school learning, do not apply in school—in particular, the rule, prevailing from birth, that basic skills (like walking and talking) are learned within important contexts established by families and neighborhood cultures. This rule is sometimes unobtrusively reinstated, however. An example has been provided by an anthropologist, Jean Lave, in collaboration with Michael Hass.[20]

Lave and Hass studied eleven children in the "upper" math group of a third-grade classroom. Over a three-week period, the teacher presented specific new techniques for carrying out multiplication and division operations, and then assigned workbook exercises that the children sat around a table doing. Hass's careful documentation of the workbook sessions showed that over the three-week period, the children gave no evidence of having adopted any of the specific strategies that the teacher presented. Instead, the children worked together to apply counting and regrouping strategies that they had previously mastered and that they knew would work for them. In addition, they invented collaborative and problem-solving procedures that the teacher apparently knew nothing about.

> The children began their group work sessions by making sure they agreed on what they were supposed to do. They coordinated the timing of their activity so as to work on approximately the same problems at the same time. They asked each other for help and helped each other without being asked. They collaborated and invented procedures. They discovered that the multiplication table printed in their book could be used to solve division problems, an opportunity for mathematical discussion of which the teacher was unaware. Each of the eleven turned in nearly errorless daily practice assignments. [They used their own counting and regrouping procedures] so as to produce the appearance of having used the teacher's procedures, for which she took a correct answer as evidence . . . The children did not take the risk of failing to get the answer right, but engaged in familiar processes . . . developing their practice of learning math in the classroom cautiously, out of known quantities. This was aimed at success or at least survival in the classroom—a specialized collection of activities— rather than being focused [as the teacher had intended] upon a deep understanding of mathematics.[21]

I've chosen this example not only because every teacher will recognize it but because every reader who has ever been in a classroom will recognize it. The learning programs that students construct, driven in part by the culture of the classroom and in part by broader social contexts, may be nothing like those their teachers expect. But this should not be an occasion for embarrassment on the part of either child or teacher. On the contrary, it demonstrates the remarkable, situation-based, spontaneous learning capabilities that humans have. We should pay more attention to these spontaneous learning systems than to anything else that happens in a classroom. Powerful forms of instruction can and should be designed to capitalize upon them.

3/ What Our Schools Should Become

Based on contemporary principles of cognitive and developmental science, a new type of schooling can be designed. It carries forward in spirit Dewey's vision of building educational programs around occupations, but is informed by systematic analyses of the mental skills that occupations involve and by current research on the best ways of fostering these skills.

Cognitive and developmental scientists, along with a great many educators, have been brooding for a long time now about how to redesign classroom instruction. Recently, many of these ideas have been pulled together and advanced by Allan Collins and John Seely Brown in a series of publications concerning what they call *"the second educational revolution."*[1] The phrase is not as immodest as it may appear. The first educational revolution, according to Collins and Brown, was the onset of formal schooling. Children were moved out of workplace apprenticeship environments and into classrooms, where reading, writing, arithmetic, and various subjects were taught in relatively abstract formats. The second educational revolution will reinstate certain apprenticeship principles that are now recognized as scientifically correct: for example, the principle that experts should work alongside children to show them what is expected.

The workplace in this case, however, is the workplace of the mind. Schooling is reconceptualized as a *cognitive* apprenticeship, a place where people go to develop skills in learning to learn, problem solving, and the creative application of ideas.

THE PRINCIPLES OF THE APPRENTICESHIP MODEL

1. *Human minds are designed for complex, situated learning.* The cognitive apparatus, the system architecture sketched in Chapter 2, did not come into existence in the abstract. It evolved, biologically, through countless episodes of real-world success and failure. Human brains are constructed to deal with richly complex environments, to make sense out of their experiences, and to store knowledge that is useful in coping with new ones.[2]

Consider how learning proceeds in everyday life—learning to ride a bicycle, for example. You may remember from your own childhood how you got on a bicycle and tried to ride it. You didn't first practice pedaling on a pedaling machine, then steering on a steering machine, and so on, until you reached some level of expertise in each separate skill, after which you began putting it all together. You just got on and tried to ride off. What you probably did instead, however, was fall off, and someone, a parent or an older child, came and helped you. They stopped the bicycle from crashing whenever you lost control of it. If you kept control of it, they stepped back, and off you went, for perhaps a yard or two, at which point they ran up and caught you again. Throughout all this, you lived in the midst of other children who were all at varying stages of expertise in riding bicycles. You probably tried out different sizes and shapes of bicycles, not to mention tricycles and scooters. There was in effect a vehicular culture of which you were an excited part. Perhaps you yearned for an elegant ten-speed and envied the teenagers who wheeled off in glittering packs.

Or consider what happened when a college freshman joins the staff of her college newspaper. Suddenly she is part of an important world of news, public personalities, writing, and production deadlines. To begin with, she is given simple jobs to do, such as cutting out clippings and filing them. But she also sits in on conferences, watches the senior reporters at work, hears the editor guiding the production process, and eventually tries her hand at interviewing and writing. When her first piece is considered for publication, it is critiqued, perhaps unkindly in her opinion, but in professional terms. This is no Mickey Mouse operation. She is part of a team that competes with other journalistic teams, and she has to learn how to keep up her end of things. When she finally sees her first published byline and begins to get approving comments from fellow students, the rewards are keen. No grade will ever mean as much.

This kind of complex, situated learning is what human brains are designed to do. The capacities are there. We can and do make sense out of a swirl of events. We can and do learn to identify important goals, cues, and strategies. It's not necessary for schools to chop learning experiences into small parcels to be practiced over brief intervals. We now know that minds learn by constructing elaborate working-memory programs for dealing with important events over long time periods. Formal education should begin, then, with the student's entry into complex, long-range learning situations that genuinely matter.

2. Expert models must participate in the instructional program. Human expertise is complicated. It cannot be obtained by adding up a list of facts to be acquired, skills to be demonstrated, and problems to be solved. Much expert knowledge is tacit: it cannot be articulated. But it can be transmitted. By working with an expert gardener you can become one yourself. The presence of experts in a learning situation is the only way to ensure that instructional objectives are fully represented.

In contrast to the behavioral objectives of traditional curriculum design, cognitive objectives are formulated from in-depth studies of experts on the subject at hand. The cognitive design of a reading program begins by asking: How do experts read? How do they deal with print? How does their attention shift? What do they think about while reading?[3] Similarly, the cognitive design of a mathematics program begins by asking: How do experts calculate? How do they solve word problems? What do experts actually do when it comes to dealing with fractions?[4]

Studies typically reveal that experts have accumulated many types of knowledge, not merely the declarative knowledge that constitutes so much academic training. Expert geologists, for example, in addition to textbook knowledge and the knowledge transmitted to them through lectures, have vast amounts of procedural knowledge. They have knowledge of drilling procedures, microscopic procedures, surveying procedures, exploratory procedures, and so on, not to mention crucial problem-solving procedures: figuring out how to find water, and where to bore. Much geological knowledge is categorical in nature—as its many terms of classification illustrate. But the procedure of sorting samples into categories—a process that often involves problem solving—is quite different from the declarative knowledge of rock categories.

A great deal of geological knowledge is also schematic in nature. Temporally, there are epochs. Spatially, there are schemas of faults, erosion patterns, and volcanic flows. Analogically, expert geologists have stored masses of sensory impressions. In their fieldwork they have scrambled over and around terrain of all sorts, and they have experienced first-hand the enormous difference between text descriptions and actual geological formations. And in the realm of logical knowledge, the expert geologist has constructed extensive theories that organize and account for phenomena—the theory of continental drift, for example.

Expert models provide the curriculum designer with guidelines and objectives. The expert has the combination of skills, knowledge of how and when to use them, and experience in using them that we want students to get a sense of and eventually gain. A variety of levels and types of expert models, may be chosen, depending on the curriculum. The professional geologist is a good model for graduate students in the field. A competent amateur geologist is an appropriate model for elementary and secondary students. But in all cases, an expert of some type must have been interviewed and studied by curriculum developers. In cognitive science, obtaining information of this kind is called *knowledge engineering*.

Although the term may have an impersonal sound to it, knowledge engineering is in fact quite personalized and humanistic. By studying expert human beings, we learn about human ways of acquiring, storing, and retrieving knowledge. We discover, for example, that feelings and motivations are part of intellectual work. We learn about work habits and work areas—how offices and laboratories are organized. We find that experts themselves never stop learning, and that they have efficient strategies for acquiring new information. Most important, we can see that expert knowledge never stands alone but is always an integral, coordinated part of complex tasks. Geologists use their knowledge to solve difficult and interesting problems, even life-saving ones. An expert demonstrates the context and ultimate purpose of learning in school.

This relates to the organization of Dewey's curriculum, but the approach is considerably more systematic than Dewey's. The point is not that a child should, say, pretend to be a farmer. Rather, educational program designers should determine what program objectives ought to be by thoroughly investigating what the expert farmer knows. The question of what type of learning experiences a child should have in order to acquire that expertise is a separate issue.

3. Education must begin where the student is. To produce a good gymnast, a coach must study the special characteristics and growth patterns of each individual student. The coach can't merely march a student through a series of preplanned exercises, grading her as she goes along, and thereby produce a champion. To produce a student who has a good grasp of American history, the same principles hold. It isn't enough to march the student through a series of preplanned lessons, grading her as she goes along. The nature of the student's preliminary understanding of history, her historical schemas, and her personal theories of how cultures change over time must be thoroughly understood. Just as the gymnastics coach can only further the development of a body that is there, so the "history coach" can only further the development of a mind that is there.

how to select and pry out unbroken pieces of slate, for example. I could swiftly categorize samples from the three types of banks. I had schemas involving what the rocks were good for. I had rudimentary theories that enabled me to make predictions—about the effects of rain and heat, for example. And of course I was well stocked with sensory images, or analogs. In other words, I was a sort of junior version of an expert.

All students entering a new domain of knowledge are, in fact, junior versions of experts. They have some of the frameworks. They have the rudiments of every type of knowledge that experts have. This is why cognitive and developmental science emphasizes the importance of basing instruction on what a beginner brings *to* a learning situation.

4. *Human learning is a social enterprise.* Roy Pea has coined the phrase *distributed intelligence* to describe the fact that expertise is typically a joint product. To deal with the many problems that building a bridge involves, for example, contributions are needed from hundreds of individuals with different skills and levels of knowledge. No individual is expected to know the same things to the same degree, as occurs in the typical classroom. Suppose classwork revolved around a joint project, to which each individual could make a unique contribution. Intelligence, in this model, instead of being held to reside in the individual, is held to reside in the group. Working together, the group can produce a brilliant collective product that no individual could have been expected to produce alone.[5]

Human learning, the accumulation of the knowledge that has produced modern civilization, is a social enterprise. It has never been the case in real life that rows of individuals, sitting behind desks, have each been charged with solving the same problem to the same level of competence. To do so in schools is not only inefficient from the standpoint of finding solutions but exceedingly poor training for the real-world learning situations that await students after their formal schooling has ended.[6]

Experts from all over the world met a decade or so ago at a conference in Rome in order to explore the profoundly complex issues of worldwide education. A report was published under the title *No Limits to Learning: Bridging the Human Gap*.[7] It began:

> Humanity is entering a period of extreme alternatives. At the same time that an era of scientific and technological advancement has brought us unparalleled knowledge and power, we are witnessing the sudden emergence of a "world problématique"—an enormous tangle of problems in sectors such as energy, population and food which confront us with unexpected complexity. Unprecedented human fulfillment and ultimate catastrophe are both possible. What will actually happen, however, depends on another major—and decisive—factor: human understanding and action.[8]

The authors attribute the crisis primarily to the failure to provide appropriate kinds of learning opportunities. Most learning, they explain, is maintenance learning. Students are taught how to maintain and perpetuate the status quo. "Maintenance learning is the acquisition of fixed outlooks, methods, and rules for dealing with known and recurring situations." Although this is certainly necessary, it is not enough. In addition, they say, there must be innovative learning—acquiring skills for dealing with new situations. Innovative learning has two main features, the conference decided: anticipation and participation.

Anticipatory learning prepares people to use techniques such as forecasting, simulations, scenarios, and models. It encourages them to consider trends, to make plans, to evaluate future consequences . . . and to recognize the global implications of local, national, and regional actions. Its aim is to shield society from the trauma of learning by shock. It emphasizes the future tense, not just the past. It employs imagination but is based on hard fact.[9]

Concerning participation, the report said:

One of the most significant trends of our time is the near-universal demand for participation. This demand is being felt on the international level as well as at national, regional, and local levels . . . Rural populations are aspiring to urban-like facilities; factory workers seek participation in management; students and faculties demand a voice in administering important school policy; women are demanding equality with men.

. . . Participation is more than formal sharing of decisions; it is an attitude characterized by cooperation, dialogue, and empathy. It means not only keeping communications open but also constantly testing one's operating rules and values; retaining those that are relevant and rejecting those that have become obsolescent.

Neither anticipation nor participation are new concepts by themselves. What is new and vital for innovative learning is the insistence that they be tied together . . . Without participation . . . anticipation often becomes futile. It is not enough that only elites or decision-makers are anticipatory when the resolution of a local issue depends on the broad-based support of some critical mass of people. And, participation without anticipation can be counter-productive and misguided.[10]

The implication for our classrooms is that participatory learning, in which students learn how to make the

most of each individual's ability for achieving an important group goal, is an essential end in itself. The typical
classroom situation, in which isolated students work
against each other competitively, rather than with each
other cooperatively, is described by the authors of *No
Limits to Learning* as downright dangerous.

THE ROLE OF THE TEACHER

In an apprenticeship learning environment—an environment in which instruction is situated in important
contexts, experts are involved, instruction begins with
the knowledge that students bring into the situation,
and intelligence is held to be a property of the group as
a whole—what is the role of the teacher?

The design of such a learning environment is a matter
of teamwork, as will be discussed in Chapter 8. A single
teacher need not be responsible for inventing the curriculums that I will be describing in the next three chapters, though that does sometimes happen. The same
principles hold that have just been described: training in
curriculum design is itself an apprenticeship. Experts of
many types should be involved, and they should assist
new teachers in building on the knowledge and expertise they bring to their own classrooms. Thanks to new
technologies, even experts who are far away can be involved.

Within the apprenticeship classroom, too, there are
students with different kinds and varying degrees of
expertise, and they can help teach one another. The
skills of teaching others and of teaching oneself—taking
responsibility for setting learning goals, setting up practice schedules, keeping track of improvement, and so
on—can be explicitly taught.

In addition, however, particular methods are useful.

These are necessitated in part by the nature of a cognitive apprenticeship, in which the skills to be taught are the mental skills of learning, thinking, and reasoning rather than the concrete skills of bicycle riding or tailoring. Mental skills may be undetectable unless they are made explicit. Collins and Brown have listed six special techniques—already familiar to many teachers—that accomplish this.

Modeling. Modeling, showing a student how something is done, enables the learner to conceptualize a sequence of processes. To model "invisible" processes such as reasoning, problem solving, knowledge retrieval, and decision making, the instructor must try to make them visible by thinking out loud, describing reasoning processes, and tracing the evolution of ideas.

A teacher who is reading aloud to students, for example, may encounter a word that will be new to most of the children. Instead of telling them what it means, the teacher might say, "Oh, here's a new word! I don't remember ever seeing that word before. Do you ever see new words when you read? Sometimes I feel a little worried when I see a new word. Do you ever feel a little worried? But then I say to myself, Now, there isn't any reason to be worried. Every word has to be new to me sometime. I didn't get born with all the words in the world in my head, so I'm going to be meeting up with new words all the time, and it's nothing to worry about. It's like an adventure. Can I figure out what a new word means? Let me see. How should I start figuring? First I'll try to say it. Maybe if I can say the word, and hear what I say, it will make me think of something it could mean. So I'll try to say the word . . . Well, that didn't help me, so I'll try something else. I'll try to figure out how the word could fit in with what I'm reading. Let's see, I just read that the horse was racing down to the beach. So maybe this word *galloping* has something to do with racing . . ." And so on. In turn, students are encouraged to follow suit and to display how they are (or could be) dealing with the problem of mastering something new.

This style of teaching makes a tremendous difference in a classroom. Instead of believing that adults have magical ways of being right, children learn that adults make mistakes, too, that they have to figure things out, too, and that acquiring knowledge is always a matter of false starts, mistakes, and slow progress. We're all in the same boat. What's important is that we help each other learn to hoist sail, steer by the stars, and bail water when necessary, not that we beat each other to the finish line.

Coaching. The student performs a task, or a portion of one, and the instructor provides guidance and feedback. Coaching may be directed toward any aspect of a working-memory program: goal setting, cue awareness, knowledge retrieval, behavior, or self-monitoring. Coaching primes or prompts a component of a working-memory program. It also helps guide and supervise practice to the point of automaticity.

Scaffolding and fading. Teachers provide support that students cannot yet provide for themselves. In the example of bike riding cited earlier, an adult or older child holds and steers the bicycle as a child learns to ride. As the child becomes progressively able to manage alone, the support is withdrawn. This is called fading. Scaffolding involves cooperative problem solving by teacher and students in more complex tasks, such as writing an essay.

Articulation. The articulation process occurs through explicit descriptions—summaries, critiques, or dialogues about situations or principles—that the instructor requires the student to produce. Having to describe something forces the student to figure out what it is. This verbal knowledge, once it is formulated, doesn't supplant nonverbal procedural or conceptual knowledge. It merely extends it by providing linguistic controls.

Reflection. Reflection is closely related to articulation. It involves comparing one's own activities to an internal model of what should have occurred. The instructional method often utilizes technology that helps students focus on particular features. A child might record himself reading aloud, for example, and then listen to the tape to decide whether he has been using correct intonation.

As a general rule, multiple forms of reflection should be available, so that the ones most helpful to a particular activity can be selected. One value of a computer is that it can trace a performance and compare it to a (previously programmed) model, thereby facilitating student reflection.

Exploration. In exploration, students are pushed into new domains of application, are required to figure out how and when their skills are relevant, and must take complete responsibility for the outcomes. Typically, exploration follows skill training, as in the Outward Bound programs, in which students spend several days alone in the wilderness after they have mastered survival techniques. In some cases, however, exploration is a useful beginning. Art instruction often begins by encouraging students to explore the nature of a new medium.

*   *   *

These six teaching methods are facilitative rather than didactic. Teachers model, prompt, coach, and encourage exploration. At the same time, they provide help and support where needed. Finally, they insist that students reflect upon what they are doing, identify important principles, and put them into words so that they can be discussed and their general applicability can be recognized.

THE MULTICULTURAL PERSPECTIVE

Internationally, nationally, regionally, and locally, education must be a shared enterprise. We are a multicultural planet. Perhaps the most important single feature of the apprenticeship school model is that it facilitates multicultural education, as can be seen by reviewing the model's principles in light of multicultural goals.[11]

First, if minds are designed for complex, situated learning, then education must take account of the natural learning environment of the student, whether it be an Indian reservation, a coastal village in Alaska, the heart of a big city, a Hispanic community, or a Vietnamese neighborhood—to mention only a few American settings. Second, if experts participate in the instructional program, then the people who specialize in the cultural history and objectives of a group will automatically be brought into the classroom setting. Third, if education begins where the student is, then it begins with the student's cultural outlook, native language, background experience, and system of personal meanings. Fourth, if the learning environment is designed as a social enterprise, then cultural background will form a natural part of each individual's contribution to a joint product.

Finally, if apprenticeship teaching methodology includes modeling, coaching, scaffolding, articulation, reflection, and exploration, then it requires decision making and problem solving by students. Such activities will raise student awareness of the fact that culture plays a role in every learning enterprise.

In multicultural curriculums today there is considerable emphasis on the holistic learning styles of native American and Hispanic groups, among others. As Robert Rhodes explains:

> [Although] there is much confusion about the term "holistic" in education . . . in this context it means a fostering of a broader base and context for understanding, a multi-level approach which encourages understanding of many aspects at the same time and of the interrelationships involved, which, in turn, encourages involvement, ownership, and commitment.[12]

In a similar vein, Manuel Ramirez and Alfredo Castaneda have described Mexican-American children as field-sensitive rather than field-independent (using abstract, analytic thinking styles), and they advocate a curriculum that "is humanized through use of narration, humor, drama, and fantasy [with emphasis upon] wholes and generalities."[13] Ramirez and Castaneda describe a field-sensitive learning environment:

> 1. Classroom is arranged for small-group instruction: small tables, rugs, and learning centers are available. This environment permits the teacher to work closely with students.
> 2. Classroom environment lends itself to group projects. It is possible for the entire class or groups to work together toward common goals.
> 3. Rooms are personalized. They reflect the ethnic and social backgrounds and interests of the students. Their class work and personal contributions decorate the walls and other areas.[14]

The field-independent learning environment has a different appearance and organization:

1. Classroom is arranged for independent activities. There are learning centers where materials are immediately available to the students, requiring minimal participation by the teacher.

2. Rooms display curriculum materials, charts, and diagrams. If children's work is displayed it consists of materials that emphasize individual achievement.[15]

Principles of apprenticeship instruction help ensure the design of holistic, field-sensitive learning environments.

Raising student consciousness of cultural pluralism is another objective of multicultural education, as James Banks emphasizes:

The multiethnic curriculum should help students develop the ability to make reflective decisions so they can resolve personal problems, and through social action, influence public policy and develop a sense of political efficacy. In many ethnic studies units and lessons, emphasis is on the memorization and testing of isolated historical facts about shadowy ethnic heroes of questionable historical significance. In these types of curricula ethnic content is merely an extension of the traditional curriculum.

The multiethnic curriculum should have goals that are more consistent with the needs of a global society . . . It is imperative that the school play a decisive role in educating citizens capable of making reflective decisions on social issues and taking effective actions to help solve them.[16]

The principles of apprenticeship teaching, and not the "memorization and testing of isolated facts," foster the type of decision making and problem solving that Banks advocates, as will become clear in the curriculum illustrations in the next three chapters.

Apprenticeship programs provide the best and most meaningful forms of education available for disadvantaged youngsters. Joe Nathan, in his book *Free to Teach*, describes a number of inner-city youth participation programs, including projects on legal rights and recourses, consumer protection, health care, vandalism reduction, and construction of safe recreational areas.[17]

As I write this, however, I mourn the state of affairs that makes it necessary for us to teach children how to deal with poverty and its attendant problems. I remember a little puppet show that was making the rounds of inner-city schools to help teach five-year-olds how to deal with rats. My heart breaks anew with the memory. Why must five-year-olds be taught how to deal with the rats? Why aren't the grown-ups dealing with the rats? By which I mean, of course, why doesn't our nation get the five-year-olds, and their families, out of rat-infested, hopelessly destructive living environments?

There is no way any school program can compensate for such environments. The best schools can hope to do is provide an oasis—a place where young minds can find nourishment and space to grow.

4/ Transmitting the Culture

In the past (and still today, in some parts of the world), the history and culture of a people existed only in its collective memory. Unless those memories were passed along to younger members of the group, no record of the people would remain on earth, except perhaps as myths.[1] In the civilized world, history and culture are transmitted in the form of written records, fashioned by hundreds of individuals who have little direct contact with those who receive what is written. Schoolchildren, in particular, have been disconnected from the personal modes of passing along a culture and have little understanding of how textbooks have become surrogates for that tradition.[2]

Educational programming exists, however, that enables children to discover and maintain real connections with their culture, from their neighborhood to their ancient origins. Such programs also provide the foundations for advanced critical analysis of historical writings—for considering the ways in which history may have been altered by the telling.

THE NEIGHBORHOOD EXPLORER

We begin with a small kit, a colorful box with a handle, labeled "The Neighborhood Explorer." It was designed by Learning About Learning (LAL), a San Antonio group whose members had backgrounds in the creative and performing arts and a strong interest in education. LAL had close and productive relations with San Antonio schools and community organizations and, over a twenty-year period, designed numerous remarkable educational projects for children.[3] The group even ran an experimental school. LAL is no longer in existence, unfortunately, since it is almost impossible for small nonprofit curriculum development organizations to survive in the multibillion-dollar world of commercial publishing.

The Neighborhood Explorer is typical of LAL's approach. The kit's subtitle is "The Next-Door, Around-the-Block, Up-and-Down-the-Building Book of Exploring, Inventing, and Imagining." Inside is a booklet that guides the collection of neighborhood data, along with pencils, map-making materials—including stickers of trees, cars, houses, and labels—and a small pad imprinted with names of items to be counted. Information about the neighborhood will be gathered quantitatively as well as qualitatively.

The materials in the Neighborhood Explorer are artfully designed to provide both scholarly and aesthetic scaffolding. They help children collect large amounts of information, and they also help them produce work that is aesthetically attractive. The importance of aesthetic scaffolding is often overlooked in programs that emphasize children's self-expression. Children usually do not have the skills to present their own images with their full beauty and meaning. Scaffolding is needed so that children are not required to display what they may view as an embarrassing mess. The involvement of trained artists who know media and who know how to provide children, no matter how inexperienced, with the materials that work for them is a critical feature of good educational programming.

The Explorer booklet begins with a section called "The Story of my Neighborhood." Scaffolding takes the form of blanks to be filled in: "My home is special because . . ." "When I look out the window I see . . ." "When I go for a walk I see . . ." "The best part of my neighborhood is . . ." Factual, descriptive data are collected, along with some value judgments. Above all, it is emphasized that what is around the children is important; they should open their eyes and look.

The child gives the same task to two or three school friends. They too write stories about the neighborhood. Together, the group begins to build a collective body of knowledge. They see throughout that point of view is everything, a sophisticated and important truth.

Facts and figures are collected in droves. Long lists must be filled in: how many animals are there in my neighborhood? How many trees are big enough to climb? How many vacant lots are there? When I stand on a street corner, how many trucks, skateboards, sports cars, joggers, go by?

What are the streets in my neighborhood named after? People? Flowers? If I invented new names for streets, what would they be? What are the signs? What new signs would I invent? What conclusions can I draw?

What are the games? What are the secret places?

When I go on a "listen" walk, do I hear cars, trucks, voices, crickets, barks, air conditioners, splashing water? What do I experience on a "smell" walk? Can I smell wet streets?

The kit has sections on lines (collecting crooked sticks, thin wires; identifying lines on buildings that are jagged, thick, diagonal), shapes, textures, colors, weather (all seasons), animals, insects, leaves, and most of all, people. A section entitled "Famous Neighbors" presents a slate of interviews designed for people who have lived in the area a long time or a short time, for people who sing, tell stories, watch birds, tell jokes, build things, take care of children, and on and on.

Finally, there is a thoughtful, integrative section: What do we do that defines neighborliness? We wave, we share holidays, we shop in the same places, we speak particular languages, we say certain kinds of things to each other. Neighborhood problems are addressed, and ways of solving them are considered. Awards are given to Great Neighbors—for helpfulness, for making beautiful windowboxes, for whatever the children think great neighbors do.

The end result of all of this, which can take months, is a neighborhood fair: the group displays the information it has collected, the problems identified, the awards bestowed, and so on. Of course the neighborhood is invited, and the turnout is usually heavy.

This project fulfills the criteria of the apprenticeship model. It moves the children directly into junior versions of the same kinds of thinking and reasoning that expert sociologists and anthropologists do. It begins where the children begin, and it guides them to build upon their own perceptions and experiences. In fact, once they've engaged in some of these simple exercises (looking for lines, for instance), they will never again look at any neighborhood in quite the same way. Once they have counted some neighborhood features for themselves, and accumulated them with the counts of others in their group, they will never again view demographic statistics as meaningless—they know that somebody once stood there and counted. Learning has been a social enterprise. Everyone has been able to do something useful and contribute to the common goal. And of course the project has been wholly situated in the children's own world.

The teaching methods described earlier are also used. With the children go teachers and visiting experts, collecting their own data and talking aloud about their plans and the reasons for those plans. Coaching is continuous, and it is guided by the materials, as are scaffolding, reflection, and articulation: mounting the fair, for example, provides numerous opportunities for extracting and discussing the basic organizing principles of the exercise. And the entire project, of course, has been exploratory in nature. Each child has to be enterprising, and each has to deal with unexpected happenings.

Above all, the project has produced reams of personal narratives, drawings, poems, and many other forms of capturing and restating metaphorically the child's personal culture. These are the same processes that preserved the culture that they will read about in textbooks and that they can experience in museums and through the study of historical documents and artifacts.

In the LAL Social Studies curriculum, older children went on to engage in some very sophisticated projects with architects and historians. They produced a book, *Lessons in Looking,* developed in collaboration with O'Neil Ford, a famous Texas architect.[4] The book includes dialogues with Mr. Ford, essays written by the youngsters, and sections such as "Sticks, Mud, and Rocks," on building materials in foreign sites and in the San Antonio area. The older students also produced their own history of Texas. They conducted interviews with elderly residents and interpreted their data under the guidance of professional historians. The link from personal narrative to formal text was explicitly made.

THE DESPERATE JOURNEY

Schools must also, of course, teach children about events that have occurred outside of their own neighborhoods and long before they were born. At the Jordanhill College of Education in Glasgow, Scotland, a team led by Fred Rendell and Patricia Watterson has produced detailed instructional guidelines for studying the Highland Clearances, a tragic period in Scottish history.

During the first part of the nineteenth century, landowners evicted thousands of small shareholding farmers (crofters) in order to make way for the more profitable enterprise of sheepherding. There is an extensive history and literature of this period, including a moving children's novel, *The Desperate Journey*, a factually based account of a family driven from their croft in Culmailie to the tenements of Glasgow and eventually to a new life in Canada. This book is the wellspring of the Rendell-Watterson curriculum.[5]

Most of the curriculum's units begin with the teacher reading aloud excerpts of the novel. The class discusses key issues and problems, and then small groups of children branch out to explore, extend, and document events. To begin with, the physical environment of Culmailie, a valley brooded over by the peaks of Ben Bhragie and Ben Lundie and edged by Dornoch Firth, must be thoroughly understood and mapped, because geography is a critical feature of the story. The family— their characteristics, their possessions, and the nature of their croft—must also be investigated and depicted.

The walls of the classroom are soon covered with giant friezes, which the children fill with trees, animals, croft buildings, people, flowers, hills, water, the family boat, and so on. Here again aesthetic scaffolding is provided. Cutting these images from cloth and other materials and affixing them to a frieze in layers produces strikingly beautiful and dramatic effects that would not be achieved if the children worked in other media that they might not yet have the skills to handle.[6]

The Jordanhill team has developed computer programs that let the children explore and simulate alternatives—to the placement of the farmhouse, for example. This program teaches them to use grid coordinates to locate the house, field, and stream and, eventually, to draw computer pictures that let them test hypotheses (about the relation of the fields to the sun, for example). The children also make models of the inside of the farmhouse and deal with the problem of fitting a family and furnishings into small places. A computer program allows them to try out possible furniture arrangements, to draw plans, and to recognize the concrete reality of fractional equivalencies.

The relationship of the traveling sun to the cottage and its windows is explored and graphed. The children chart the sequence of the farming year and the amount of time that must be spent on various activities—digging, fishing, harvesting, and the like. This leads to a section on hands and tools, and a computer program that permits children to animate their ideas about tool functions.

Writing is part of all these activities, both on and off the computer. Data files are kept. Writing exercises include both reports on the classwork that has been done and elaborations of the story. Here is a poem written by several children together:

SUMMER IN CULMAILIE

The sun burns in the clear blue sky
Faraway mountains with snowy peaks
Trees stand on the rounded hills
The screech of seagulls flying over the Lundie Burn

> The salt smell of the wind blows from the sea
> James Murray is working hard in his fields
> He tastes sweat on his lips
> His empty boat lies on the shore
> The Murrays are happy here.[7]

The Murrays' happiness is suddenly destroyed when they are evicted from their croft by the owner of the land, who can get more money for it through sheepherding. This shocking event leads the students and their teachers into a discussion of the difficult and intricate issues of land rights and ownership. The issues have become intuitively meaningful and compelling to the children, who would otherwise be unable to deal conceptually with the esoteric matters of common law and land grants. The children begin to examine original historical sources: narratives written at the time, accounting documents, legal orders, and trials. All such material is now alive with meaning. The children also use computer census files to investigate and compare population changes that occurred in Golspie (Culmailie), Glasgow, and Canada. These population movements become dramatically real to them as they reconstruct the migration of the Murray family.

Many factors have to be considered: where should the Murrays go? How will they get there? What will they take with them? How will they find their way? What dangers will they encounter? In the course of all this, collages, topographical maps, daily journals, and drawings are produced, and the geography of Scotland is thoroughly explored. Because the Murrays go by fishing boat down the west coast, coastal areas and islands are also studied in detail.

Life in the nineteenth-century tenements and factories of Glasgow was vivid and shocking. The Murray children must to go work in the weaving mills, because there is no work for their parents. This is an especially compelling way to lead children into the study of economic issues that they would otherwise find difficult and uninteresting. Why were there jobs for children, and not for adults? Why were children cheaper to hire? How did it change a family when the children, rather than the parents, became the breadwinners?

While never losing touch with the human drama, the teacher in addition guides the class in gaining skills in literary, historical, and sociological analysis. What kinds of words, for example, fit Glasgow that would not have fit Culmailie? The students respond:

> hard shiny cobbles
> great stone-arched bridge
> tall chimney stalks smoking

How will the city be affected by the smoke and the prevailing winds? Which part of the city will be grimy? What makes noise in machines? Computer programs let children invent and predict machine functions, explore weaving patterns, and simulate the economic outcomes of various factory schedules and costs.

In subsequent sections the family's life continues. Eventually they manage to emigrate to Canada, where they live happily ever after. Though part of a specific time and place, the topic is universal. The approach lays the foundation for more advanced study in the social sciences and it is clear also that this type of curriculum teaches widely generalizable skills and schemas for learning. Classes soon become remarkably self-sufficient. Children acquire a large stock of diversified techniques that can be applied to new topics. They have learned what to expect of computers and what they can be used for: graphic studies, word processing, simulations, data storage, and searches. They have learned how to locate and examine historical documents, and what kinds of documents are going to be available. They have learned to express their personal reactions and values through stories, poems, paintings, and constructions. They have learned map-making, topographical, and scale-drawing techniques. They have learned techniques of literary analysis, methods of tracing sociological implications, and techniques of simulating economic outcomes. Imagine what kinds of informed and competent citizens our nations might produce if we provided social studies education of this type, integrated over a twelve-year period and culminating during the last two or three years of high school in the investigation of contemporary problems and in internships in adult problem-solving environments.

KINGS AND THINGS

Before returning to America, let me sketch another Scottish project, this one designed to help students master what can be a deadly dull subject: the history of the British monarchy.

In the Desperate Journey curriculum, children represent their ideas in art media as valuable supplements to verbal exposition. If children can draw a picture of what they know, make a poem about it, and display it in some concrete form, they have truly made that knowledge their own. They are not merely parroting someone else's words but have presented the information in their own terms.

Skills in the arts are also important objectives in themselves, and the next curriculum incorporates training in acting, singing, dancing, costume design, and ceramics in addition to training in historical research and writing. Kings and Things originated as a musical comedy that was broadcast over BBC Radio for Schools.[8] One school that received it was in the town of Stornoway on the island of Lewis, the largest of the Outer Hebrides Islands off the northwest corner of Scotland. Roderick Grant, a teacher, sent for the script, and his class spent the spring of 1980 engaged in projects that culminated in a production of the musical "Kings and Things" for the whole town.

Each student was assigned a historical character, usually a monarch. That student was responsible for thoroughly researching the character and writing up the results. The class, in other words, produced its own history book.

Students learned skills of costume design, from research to the preparation of models to the actual construction of the costumes they would wear. In addition, students produced paper sculptures—masks—and ceramic mugs of their characters. These projects, too, required research. History shapes art, as art shapes history. Indeed, Kings and Things makes this point explicitly—for example, that the Tudors, through the genius of William Shakespeare, dramatically altered views of Richard III.

The musical takes place in a waxworks museum. Moving through it are some students, accompanied by a professor. As they comment on the monarchs they see, the wax characters come to life and talk back to them. Some of the monarchs join the tour, and the characters talk to each other. This simple scenario makes possible all sorts of scholarly and theatrical dialogue. As a not-so-trivial part of the production, many retrieval cues are provided for keeping the royal succession straight. The four King Georges, for example, perform a delightful number that includes the following verses:

If I were not King George the First
a linguist I would be.
I don't speak English, not at all,
I was born in Germany.
As an English-Hanoverian King,
the first one of my kind
I'd be an English-speaking king,
with accent so refined.

If I were not King George the Second
I don't know what I'd be.
I have no interests, not at all,
a complete nonentity.
An English-Hanoverian King
the second my line,
I'd be a fascinating king,
and brilliantly I'd shine.

If I were not King George the Third,
a farmer I would be.
I'd plant my turnips everywhere,
as far as the eye can see.
As an English-Hanoverian king,
the third one from the stable,
I'd be an agricultural king,
with interests vegetable!

If I were not King George the Fourth,
a builder I would be.
Constructing bijou palaces,
especially by the sea.
As an English-Hanoverian king,
the fourth one (and the best!)
I'd be an architect king,
in my gas-lit, gilded nest![9]

According to the script, the four kings "link arms and perform a little dance."

Kings and Things illustrates a trend that will play a

key role in the schools of the 1990s: use of communications technologies for distance education. Satellite, cable networks, video and radio facilities, computer networks, not to mention telephone, facsimile, and postal services, are bringing expert curriculum designers and teachers into contact with students all over the world. The authors of Kings and Things were based in London, and they worked in collaboration with history scholars from British universities. In a few more years it will be common for teachers like Roderick Grant to be in daily contact with such educational resource centers to receive direct guidance and encouragement. Further, classrooms will eventually transmit back to their educational support services, so that students can show their progress to date and receive new suggestions. Most important, students and teachers will be directly linked to other classrooms working on the same production. What is coming into existence are wide, cooperating, apprenticeship environments linked through electronic networks, all being coached and supported by central teams of experts who would never otherwise be so widely available.[10]

DARK CAVES, BRIGHT VISIONS

A few years ago, the Metropolitan Museum in New York hosted a spectacular display of art and artifacts left by our late Ice Age ancestors 35,000 years ago.[11] Since prehistoric symbology is a research interest of mine, I hastened to the exhibit, as did tens of thousands of schoolchildren, brought to the museum on field trips. Observing them afforded interesting examples of the distinction between a type of schooling that presents information to students in administratively tidy units and a type of schooling that views students as junior experts, apprentices in a shared intellectual enterprise.

On the day that I was there, most of the school groups were moved, a class at a time, from one exhibit to the next, pausing before each to hear a lecture from a guide or teacher. Since an entire group stopped at the same time before the same exhibit, it was not possible for everyone to see or hear. And even if the lectures could be heard, they were relatively meaningless to children who lacked any real understanding of the time vistas involved or of the significance of a bit of bone to an abstruse archaeological theory. Groups were restless, therefore, and crowd control was the teacher's primary concern, especially since some of the hallways were dark in order to heighten the cave illusions. One hallway was also raised, and each group instantly discovered that it could make booming noises by tramping hard over the hollow areas—booms that could never be proved to have been produced by any particular pair of feet. This seemed to provide the main entertainment of the day.

There were two classes, however, one of junior high school students and the other of second graders, which did not fit that mold. I became aware of these children when one or two of them materialized beside me, studying an exhibit with a quiet intensity that equaled my own and making notes and drawings, as I was. Eventually, I discovered that the adult who offered them advice from time to time was their teacher. Each teacher, however, was enjoying the exhibit on a relatively uninterrupted basis, with absolutely no concern for discipline or control.

The junior high students had packets of worksheets, which contained questions about issues and problems that the students had come to the exhibit to resolve. Some questions were factual, but most required inference and thought. The students had to figure out for themselves where and what the evidence would be concerning particular questions. They could work together, and they consulted among themselves frequently, but always in tones that were in no way disturbing—theirs were quiet, excited conversations. Clearly the students had been extensively prepared for the exhibit. (I would hope this had even included participating in some digs themselves, though I had no information about that.) They were provided with scaffolding in their worksheets that was not unlike the structure of questions, or "mental worksheet," that an adult brings to such an exhibit. In a few more years, these students would be able to do the same thing without any assistance.

The second graders also had worksheets, but in their case the sheets were plain pieces of paper affixed to small clipboards. Their assignment was quite simple: draw a picture of anything that interests you and write a little something about it. The emphasis here, quite rightly, was on heightening the children's awareness of the visual beauties and mysteries that were all around them. The children knew these were things that had been "left behind" by people who lived a long time ago. They also knew that no one was sure what these things were or what they meant. The children were to make their own records and to speculate freely and imaginatively.

It was fascinating to see what the children chose to study. Some were attracted by shapes and lines; they drew pictures of bones and artifacts with holes in them. Some were attracted by patterns; they copied dots and geometric designs. Some were attracted by function: beads, needles, and spearheads were popular items. The highlight of my visit, in fact, was standing before an exhibit of a necklace of bone and shell that had been found on a 30,000-year-old skeleton. In front of me, raptly copying the necklace, were two seven-year-olds. For at least ten minutes we stood there. I studied the engravings on the necklace, speculating on their symbolism; they drew forms, counting each piece and paying close attention to relative sizes. I don't know which of us could be said to have learned the most. For me, it was what all education ought to be, a time of ageless, shared intellectual joy.

FURTHER APPLICATIONS

These four programs are generic in their underlying form, and many different versions could be generated. The Neighborhood Explorer was initially developed for the San Antonio Mexican-American community, but it would work equally well in Appalachian, native American, Scottish, Japanese, and other communities, and in the inner city. The program in each case would be developed in collaboration with experts in the particular culture, and there would be adaptations—in interviewing techniques, for example.

The Desperate Journey has occurred in so many different cultures that it has almost a mythic quality. We might be talking about a native American tribe, Australian pioneers, Louisiana Acadians, or the Vietnamese boat people.

Kings and Things is but one monarchical sequence. A similar program could focus on Japan, on African tribes, or on the different forms of leadership in Scottish clans and the United States. The principles here, of using art media to depict and remember history and of examining ways in which art and history influence each other, will remain the same.

The "Dark Caves, Bright Visions" exhibit illustrates the most generic case of all: our common human heritage from which contemporary cultural diversity has only recently evolved.

The curriculums described in this chapter and the next may remind some readers of those developed in the 1960s. Man, A Course of Study, for example, a remarkable anthropology curriculum developed under Jerome Bruner's direction, is still available.[12] How are the curriculums I have described any different? A similar question was put to Bruner: how are your programs different from Dewey's? And Dewey must have been queried about Rousseau.[13]

The answer is the same in all cases: knowledge advances in spirals. Classical concepts are continually reintegrated in more contemporary formats. Added in are new concepts and supporting evidence. Today we have extensive new evidence about brain function, mental processes, and growth patterns—scientific facts that were not previously known, though they were foreshadowed and intuitively recognized by some. We know now beyond any doubt that effective education must be designed to fit and advance the complexity of children's minds.

5/ Science and Technology

To teach science and technology, the educational system must capitalize on the human fascination with how things work. With enormous drive and energy, humans have always sought to find out not only how things work but how to make them work better, and they have invented tools of every sort to aid them in their search. Tools, with their infinite, magical potential, are the greatest playthings on earth. "My toys are all tools," Henry Ford said, "they still are. And every fragment of machinery a treasure."[1]

We see this fascination with how things work recapitulated in every growing child.[2] The failure of the formal educational system to capitalize on these enormous energies is perhaps the most striking anomaly of schooling. If it looks like play it can't be education, our schools seem to say. Yet at its best, discovery is akin to play. Scientific problem solving, as described by experts, often begins with a sense of wonder and excitement. It also involves intense observation, pondering, prediction, and testing—something close to an obsession driven by deep curiosity. There are many techniques that must be learned and practiced, of course, but the heart of science is the drive to discover, not the mastery of laboratory procedures and report formalities or the ability to recite facts from textbooks. Many important advances in science and technology take place in informal apprenticeship environments in laboratories around the world, and we need to design such environments for our children as well.[3] School science—the preparation of a scientifically literate citizenry—should involve students in problems of real importance and require them to accept responsibility for serious problem solving on their own.

A SKYE PLANTATION

Situated in the heart of a rolling moor on the Isle of Skye, Macdiarmid School comprises several stone cottages, interconnected and painted a fresh light yellow. Between thirty and forty children are distributed through grades 1 to 7. At recess, the students scramble over the hillocks and perch on top of them to eat their snacks.

Local environmental issues were of great concern to Philip Brown, Head Teacher at the school when I visited. During the Highland Clearances, the farms on Skye had been destroyed. Then in World War I, because of the need for fuel to support British troops, most of the island's forests were also destroyed. The weather, wet but not overly cold, favored the buildup of peat, a vegetative matter that does not fully rot. Peat is a spongy substance, sometimes hard enough to hold up houses, people, and animals and sometimes soggy enough to suck them under. Trees can grow in peat, but on Skye the sheep, of which there had come to be countless numbers, ate the shoots that would otherwise have resulted in reforestation. The forestry service was doing a good deal of replanting, but only in regimented pines, not in naturally occurring varieties such as ash and birch. The main problem, Brown felt, was to raise the consciousness of children. Although some history texts described how the peninsula of Trotternish (the school lies at its base) had once been so thickly forested that cows had to wear bells so they could be located in the late afternoon, no adults even remembered that forests had once existed on the island.

Brown and his schoolchildren selected a patch of land that was especially stony and useless, even for sheep, and requested permission of the laird to plant trees on it. Permission was granted, and the children planted trees on what is now called the Plantation.

Over the years the students have kept extremely detailed scientific records of what was happening—growth of the trees, changes in the soil, new plants that appeared, birds and animals that came, insects and diseases, and the effects of the weather. The records have been bound into books that include photographs, illustrations, and specimens. Everything that could be counted or measured or weighed is put into tables and graphs. Detailed entries are still made daily.

There have been many occasions for excitement. One year, for example, a sandpiper made her nest in the Plantation. As luck would have it, the children happened to be on hand the day the eggs hatched. Baby sandpipers are off and running from the moment of hatching, and in this case every hatchling had a stream of joyous children running after it. The class books of this period contain a great many moulted sandpiper feathers.

The Plantation has also been the occasion for learning about the sociology of environmental studies. Parents and other adults were not uniformly enthusiastic about the project when it first began. It was common knowledge among the adults that trees wouldn't grow on the moors. Brown was disputing that, and there was concern that he might be teaching the children to distrust their elders.

With time, however, the adults came to accept the Plantation and its message. Now among the populace, even among the crustiest skeptics, it is said that this is, after all, a good school for children to go to, because soon they will have trees to climb.

SHADOWS

At the University of Delaware the College of Education has a Curriculum Development Laboratory. Its director, Deborah Smith, has developed curriculums for the scientific education of young children.[4] Her approach is described as a *conceptual change* curriculum.[5]

Conceptual change curriculums have grown out of the work of Jean Piaget, who said frequently that knowledge cannot be put into students' heads by teachers but must be constructed from within by the students themselves. In terms of the typology of knowledge described in Chapter 2, Piaget was stressing the importance of procedural, conceptual, analogical, and logical knowledge—forms of knowledge that come into existence through the actions and experiences of students—as opposed to declarative knowledge, which is imparted through the words of teachers and books.

How to stimulate the development of nondeclarative knowledge is an important issue in the Piagetian literature. Piaget believed that such knowledge was stimulated naturally by events that contradicted a student's preconceptions. Curriculums based on Piaget's theory thus set up situations that puzzle and challenge students.[6]

A conceptual change curriculum begins with the assessment of a child's intuitive ideas about a phenomenon, and then provides the child with experiences that challenge these conceptions. To cope with the challenge, the child must invent or construct new explanations. This produces new logical knowledge, which comes into existence only when students reason something out for themselves.

One of the curriculums that Smith has developed concerns the properties of light and shadows. The unit begins when the teacher interviews the children to determine the nature of their understanding. The interview questions include:

Someone told me that the shadow is like a reflection in a mirror of you. Could that be true?

Another kid told me that the sun pushes your shadow out of you. What do you think? Could that be true?

When it's nighttime, and you're in bed and all the lights are turned off, do you have a shadow?

Another kid told me your shadow was inside you at night. Could that be true?

The interview typically elicits various types of misconceptions from young children (see Table 3). They generally believe that a shadow is a concrete substance that comes from inside the body, is projected outward from the front, exists in the dark, and is something like a reflection in a mirror.[7]

Daily activities are planned to challenge these beliefs. For the first lesson, a teacher brings in a light and a basket of objects with interesting shapes, and the children address such questions as: what kinds of things have shadows? Only humans? Animals? Objects? Do all objects have shadows? How about the ones in this basket? Can we predict what their shadows will look like?

Table 3 Examples of children's misconceptions about light and shadows

Children's ideas	Scientific explanations
The shadow is a concrete object or substance.	Shadows are the result of the absence of light, not the presence of anything.
A shadow comes from inside the body, and is projected outward from the front or face.	Shadows occur when light travels from a source in all directions and is blocked in some way.
Shadows exist without the light; at night, they are still present either on the floor or inside your body.	Shadows require light; they cannot be present at night (night itself is a shadow, the absence of light).
Shadows are like your reflection in the mirror.	Shadows differ from reflections in that reflections are the result of bouncing of light that continues traveling; shadows result from the blocking of light. Mirror images reveal color and details of the object; shadows do not.

The teacher next turns the objects in different ways, and the children revise their predictions. This is often quite exciting for the children, and leads to the selection of objects whose shadows are hard to predict and might fool others. The children must articulate their reasoning and justify their predictions. An experiment is tried. Out of the class's sight, a light is set up, an object is placed before it, and someone traces around the shadow. The tracing is then presented to the class, which tries to guess what the object was. Guessers must explain exactly what their reasoning is based upon. The class then breaks up into groups to produce more "foolers," which are presented at a final meeting. If no one guesses an object correctly, then the children who present the tracing must re-create their procedures as proof that the object was its source. Books of "fooler recipes" are eventually produced. Here is one by a child named Meredith:

Recipe for Foolers

a object

light

a screen

and a friend

Make a shadow of one object in 3 different positions. Then trace your shadow on white paper and glue your shadows on black paper. Pick some objects that you think would make a similar shadow and put them in a row. Call a friend and ask them which object they think made the shadows! Have fun!

The daily lessons are designed so that over time, the children collect evidence demonstrating that their preconceptions do not generate accurate predictions. Eventually a more advanced theory of light and shadow is constructed by the group—an example of "distributed intelligence" in action. Children gradually come to understand that a shadow results when light is blocked, that light is emitted in all directions, that mirror images result from bouncing light, not from blocked light, and so on. From the reports of first-graders we may infer the types of challenges, predictions, and surprises involved (see Figure 4). (I was glad to note that no one challenged

April. 2 3, 1985.
We had two lights
and we had two
Shadow. When we
put on the two
lights.

May 2, 1985.
we found out when
a object is in front
of a mirror it did
show color.
The shadow did not show
color.

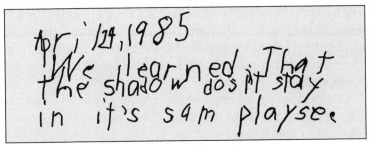

Apr, 124, 1985

We learned That
the shadow dosn't stay
in it's sam playse.

4. (*above and facing*) Science reports by young children.

the belief, revealed in one of the drawings, that shadows smile.)

The classroom is designed for a variety of activities: group meetings, experimenting, tracing, computing, and writing up results (older children use word processors). The daily science lessons, which last about one and a half hours, follow a regular pattern, and the children gradually acquire scripts or schemas for the different parts of it. The children learn to expect puzzlers, to make predictions, to deal with contradictions, and to search for resolutions. They often summarize and review. They work at experiments in pairs and sometimes assist the teacher in monitoring other children by asking them challenging questions. After a few weeks, it is clear that the children are learning to think like scientists. The classroom has taken on the atmosphere of a research center, where colleagues are excitedly participating in joint discoveries.

NAUTICAL STUDIES

The town of Stromness is on the largest of the Orkney Islands, at the top of Britain. Its narrow, stone-paved main street is not far from the water, and the rest of the town rises steeply, as if terraced. At the top of the hill is Stromness Academy, a six-year secondary school. Many such public schools in the Scottish isles are called academies, and some of them are free boarding schools. Pupils from even more remote, rural areas live in school dormitories during the week and return home only on weekends.

Stromness Academy specializes in nautical training. The program's designer and head is Captain Robert Sutherland, a former seaman who is also certified as a teacher. Pupils at the academy are provided with varying degrees of training in seamanship and navigation, and they also learn how to swim. The need for the program arose from the fact that many people who live on the islands, Sutherland found, are terrified of water and are superstitiously afraid of acquiring strategies for surviving in it. The North Sea is of course extremely cold, and there is probably some truth to the islanders' belief that even those who can swim do not survive long in its waters. Nevertheless, Sutherland has set about making everyone who comes through the high school nautically literate. His curriculum has required a great deal of advance planning, including the development of an extensive set of materials, but much of the day-to-day operation of the program falls to the students themselves.

The academy owns a 45-foot launch, a 20-foot Orkney yawl, a 27-foot whaler, and a number of dinghies. An Orkney North Isles skiff has also been fitted out with traditional rig. Throughout the day a visitor will find busy students piling in and out of boats, practicing rowing, sailing, or taking off in the launch. In a special building by the water there are student work stations, filled with practice knots, nets in progress, and navigation problem sets.

During their first two years, in addition to learning how to swim (in an indoor pool), all students engage in boat-work training from Easter to the end of September, learning steering, anchoring, and practical seamanship. During the winter, when it is too stormy to go out in the boats, students study seamanship on land, including sea terms, elementary navigation, and rope work.

By the third year, a number of students will begin working in one of three courses of instruction. In the Vocational course, students cover the syllabus for deck-boy training and entry into the fishing industry. They study general seamanship, elementary boat-handling, boat construction, and navigational rules. Considerable time is devoted to rope and canvas work, basic net making, and maintenance of the boats. There is also a ten-week unit on cooking aboard ship. Through this very practical course of training, Sutherland trains his Vocational students to be the best deck-boys in Scotland.

A second set of pupils, about 35 percent of the total student body, studies for Scottish Certificates (Ordinary Grade) in either Navigation, or Seamanship and Nautical Knowledge. The Navigation syllabus covers earth measurement; the various sailings—parallel, plane, mean and middle latitude; how to construct a Mercator Chart and calculate course and distance; basic time measurement and theory of astronomical position line navigation; how to determine a vessel's position by astronomical observations; chartwork and pilotage; tides; and navigational instruments. The syllabus for Seamanship and Nautical Knowledge covers basic ship construction and the main types of merchant ships; boat and ship maintenance; tonnage; stability and trim calculations; construction; care and use of rope; principles of simple purchases; direction on the earth's surface; instruments used on board ship; anchoring; maneuvering and berthing; tides and tidal streams; meteorological instruments and weather study; and the sea and the British economy.

A third, smaller group of students pursues the Higher Grade, a more theoretical course of study in Navigation. This includes everything listed for the Ordinary course, plus spherical geometry and more advanced meteorology and navigational astronomy.

Having mastered formidable bodies of knowledge, both the Ordinaries and the Highers sit for examinations in their fifth or sixth year. Figure 5 contains some examples of their examination questions. The Highers go on for advanced degrees at universities. Despite their rural and isolated locations, Scottish academies send more graduates to universities than any other secondary training institutions in Britain.

TOOLS FOR THOUGHT

Computers play a number of important roles in education. First, they enable students to deal with data in formats that are more flexible, meaningful, and efficient than those provided by pencil and paper. We saw several examples in the Desperate Journey curriculum, in which students used computers to investigate local topography and the dimensions of rural and urban dwellings, to access census data, and to study how a change in one or more variables in a cotton mill—labor costs, raw material costs, time, profit margins—could affect outputs and profits. They even simulated weaving patterns and discovered how changes in threads, colors, and pattern dimensions would look. These are all ways in which adult professionals use computers.

A second important role of computers is to teach, which they do in two primary ways: they provide practice environments, and they provide environments for discovery. In both cases, computers make possible a

Seamanship & Nautical Knowledge (Ordinary Grade)

The question is about lifesaving, and you will have four minutes in which to answer it. (Show the following picture.)

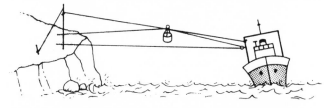

(Now say:) The sketch shows a ship aground off a cliff. Describe how the people ashore and the crew on the ship rigged this breeches buoy.

Navigation (Higher Grade)

The map below shows the pressure distribution at a particular time. With reference to the map compare and contrast the weather conditions being experienced in the Moray Firth at A, off Oban at B, and to the west of the Hebrides at C, commenting on wind strength and direction, sea state, visibility, air temperature and barometric tendency.

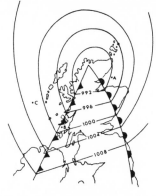

5. Examination questions in nautical studies.

more individualized and more closely monitored learning environment.

Computer-based practice environments. Computers have played a key role in a University of Delaware curriculum for reading, writing, and spelling. I will focus on the part played by the computer here, and describe the program itself more fully in the next chapter. The skills to be learned through this curriculum are quite complex, and children need to practice them far more than classroom schedules typically allow. The computer provides an attractive and efficient practice medium. The program is designed, therefore, so that instruction can be shared by teacher and computer—the teacher doing what she does best, and the computer doing what it does best. The computer component of this computer-shared instruction is the CompEtc family of programs: it includes CompSpell, CompWrite, and CompRead, among others.

In CompSpell, the student practices individualized lists of spelling words selected by the student and teacher in consultation. An important facet of all the CompEtc programs is that students learn to accept responsibility for their own learning. They identify their own strengths and weaknesses, decide what needs to be practiced and how long to practice it, and print their own records of achievement.

In the CompSpell practice exercises, a digitized speech program dictates words to the student through earphones. The student types each word as he hears it. The computer won't let him make a mistake. If he types the wrong letter, the computer displays a dash, and won't allow the student to continue until he figures out what is correct. This prevents the student from reading and thus unintentionally practicing and reinforcing his own incorrect spelling. A teacher could never be quick enough to stop a student from writing down wrong letters, even if she were sitting beside him, much less while she is managing a whole class. But in a computer class, each student's machine can prevent errors. Further, each student can practice an individualized set of words that are of interest and importance to him.

Such uses of computers take advantage of their strengths and free teachers to concentrate on other aspects of the program. In teaching spelling, for example, teachers will use their skills and insights to teach strategies for analyzing spelling words. It is much better for a teacher to do this than for curriculum designers to try to program a computer to do it.

When students make errors during spelling practice, they can usually figure out how to correct them. If not, they can ask to have the word repeated, pronounced in a more distinct way, flashed to them, or they can ask the teacher, who will be circulating and coaching, for a clue. The teacher might ask, for example, "What's the final *e* rule that could work here?" The computer, meanwhile, keeps a record of the students' errors and their repetition and flash requests, and prints them out at the end of the session. The computer also recycles words that a student has missed. A word must be spelled correctly three times before it is deleted from a student's list.

CompWrite provides an environment for handwriting practice. The computer models the production of a letter by writing it, so to speak, with an invisible hand. This is something a teacher cannot do without covering up parts of the letter. Young children put their finger on the screen and trace the letter as it appears, pacing themselves to match the computer. When the match is right, it looks as if the child is drawing the letter on the computer screen with her finger. This is quite a fascinating task for a young child, simple though it is. It trains the child's brain to move the hand at a steady tempo, which is one key to good handwriting. As the child's skill increases, the computer's writing speed can be increased. The child will be involved in that judgment. "Should we speed it up?" the teacher will ask, thus helping the child learn how to evaluate a developing skill and to accept responsibility for it. CompWrite can also present groups of letters and whole words, when children are ready for them. The program can print or it can write in cursive.

In CompRead, text is displayed, and children read it aloud or silently. A cursor can be advanced either by the reader or by the teacher. (The cursor is an underline, or sometimes a change in color—to red, for example.) The cursor can be advanced word by word or phrase by phrase. In the latter case, color will flow across each phrase, which encourages the child to read several words as a unit.

In another version of the program, a single word can be displayed on a letter-by-letter or syllable-by-syllable basis. The delays between letters or syllables are very short, a matter of milliseconds. But they provide just enough time for brain processes to deal with one letter (or syllable) before having to deal with the next one. In ordinary reading, until the child learns how to manage her attention, too much print may come into her mind at once. When text is presented on the computer, that overload can be prevented. It is astonishing how much easier reading feels when these very tiny amounts of extra processing time are allowed.

CompRead programs are doing what no one else can do for the reader—perceptually highlighting whole phrases at a time and displaying print at variable rates. The teacher will be doing what the computer cannot do—discussing the meaning of the text and helping the children evaluate their growing skills.

Computer-based discovery environments. The Thinker-Tools Project is a curriculum developed by Barbara White and her colleagues.[8] It is another example of a conceptual change curriculum, like the Shadows curriculum described above. In this case, the topic is Newtonian mechanics, and the students are sixth graders.

Young children have some quaint ideas about physical phenomena. Older children and adults have some quaint ideas, too. Many of us, for example, believe (from experience with car accelerators, among other things) that it takes a constant force to produce a constant velocity. The truth, however, is that a force causes a change in velocity, and a constant force produces a constant acceleration.

This may seem simple enough, and it can easily be demonstrated, but it requires an assumption that ought to be questioned: why are the forces additive? As White points out, there are other ways in which a new velocity might interact with an existing velocity. For example, the new velocity could override the object's initial velocity; the two velocities could fight for control of the object, and one of them could win, or there could be a compromise; or the new velocity could take turns with the initial velocity.

As in the Shadows curriculum, the ThinkerTools curriculum requires students to resolve such challenges through experimentation. But rather than using concrete materials, ThinkerTools provides a microworld—a computer environment—for experimentation.

An example of one such microworld appears in Figure 6. The student must control the motion of an object

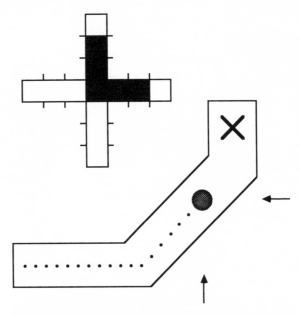

6. Some components of the ThinkerTools microworld.

so that it navigates a track and stops on the target, X. The shaded dot can be thought of as a spaceship, a billiard ball, or a molecule. The student manipulates a joystick that will guide the object in either an up-down or a left-right direction. To move the object, the student must press a "fire" button on the joystick. This distinguishes the direction of a force from the application of a force, an important theoretical principle. If the student continues to press the fire button, the impulse will be repeated at fixed intervals (¾ of a second). This repetition can be altered so that, for example, the student can apply smaller impulses at a faster rate. Ways of introducing friction and gravity also exist in the microworld.

The large cross in the middle of the figure is called the

datacross. It is something like a pair of crossed "thermometers" that depict horizontal and vertical velocities. If the dot is given a large upward velocity, and gravity is acting, the datacross will begin with a large amount of "mercury" in the upward direction. This amount will gradually reduce to zero (because of the effects of gravity) and will then increase in the downward direction. The datacross trains the student to "see" velocity graphically.

By means of a series of experiments, students discover such principles as: an impulse to a moving object, if applied in the same direction that the object is moving, adds to its speed; an impulse applied in the opposite direction subtracts from its speed; quantitative predictions can be made using familiar arithmetical functions (this may be the first time that many students realize that they have the ability to use mathematics inventively); when an impulse is applied to an object, its velocity is changed; laws developed for horizontal dimensions work equally well in vertical dimensions; horizontal and vertical dimensions are independent of one another—an upward or downward impulse will not affect horizontal velocity; however, vertical and horizontal velocity components will combine (by vector addition) to determine speed and direction of an object; and continuous forces, like gravity, can be thought of as a lot of small impulses applied in sequence. Eventually, the students discover simple versions of fundamental laws such as Force = mass × acceleration.

Exercises are introduced in the same way they were in the Shadows curriculum. The teacher leads the class in a general discussion of a problem and elicits predictions from the class. Students are then sent off to test their predictions and prepare reports. Students usually work in pairs or small teams.

An extremely important part of the ThinkerTools curriculum is the formalization phase. In their microworld exercises, students have discovered and formulated principles or laws that account for their findings—for example, "If you keep giving the dot impulses in the direction that it's going, it keeps speeding up." Students must learn to evaluate the ways in which such laws can be stated and to choose the best formulation. The form of a law is thus examined to make sure it is general, yields precise predictions, and is stated in the simplest possible terms.

White found that after two months of this training, sixth graders show, on tests, more sophisticated understanding of Newtonian mechanics than do high school students—students who are six years older and who have taken a traditional physics course. In addition, the sixth graders have learned how to use computers in the ways that physicists and mathematicians use them.

The complete ThinkerTools curriculum is far more extensive than I have illustrated here. Students can design their own experiments; define other objects (such as walls) and give them additional properties (mass, position, color, elasticity); set up crashes, explosions, and bounces; and introduce more dots and set up attractions among them. Timers and counters can be displayed. Time can also be "frozen," in order to inspect a datacross or make a prediction. Even the frame of reference can be changed, so that one dot, for example, can be examined from the "point of view" of another. Entire new microworlds, having special properties, can be created. The students are provided with a powerful vehicle for understanding how the processes of inquiry evolve in the minds of scientists.

Computers and apprenticeship. I have discussed only a few of the many points that can be made about the value of learning environments that include computers, particularly as related to the apprenticeship model. Allan Collins and John Seely Brown have written about this in much greater detail.[9] Even from the few examples here, however, it is clear that computers are valuable aids in apprenticeship teaching techniques: modeling, coaching, scaffolding and fading, and requiring students to reflect, articulate, and explore.

CompText, for example, models phrase-by-phrase reading, by moving the cursor according to the rhythm of an expert reader. ThinkerTools models physical principles that cannot easily be extrapolated from everyday experience.

In CompSpell the computer serves as a coach, "locking on" to a student, remembering perfectly every move the student makes, and maintaining infinite patience. Help provided by a computer coach occurs the instant the student needs it, not when a busy teacher can manage to schedule it amid many students and duties.

Scaffolding and fading are illustrated in CompWrite: the child manually follows the "unfolding" of a letter on the screen. Similarly, the datacross in ThinkerTools scaffolds the child's growing understanding of graphs.

When ThinkerTools represents the motion of the dot by changing the height of the "mercury" in the datacross, it enables the student to reflect on his velocity manipulations. Both articulation and reflection are fostered when CompSpell requires students to state reasons for their spelling decisions, and when ThinkerTools requires students to state reasons why some principles are more elegant than others. Note, however, that only humans—teachers or other students—can effectively monitor verbal articulation, at least until computers are much better at understanding natural language. Computers and humans need to share instruction.

ThinkerTools, in enabling children to construct new microworlds of their own, illustrates the role computers can play in encouraging exploration. We have also seen how computers facilitated exploration in the Desperate Journey curriculum.

Computers should be incorporated into comprehensive programs of instruction. They should not be, as they so often are, tangential. Nor should they be thought of as replacements for human teachers. Computers are empowering devices for human minds engaged in the human enterprise of learning.

FURTHER APPLICATIONS

The four curriculums reviewed here illustrate apprenticeship programs in areas of science and technology. These illustrations, like those in the previous chapter, should be thought of as generic. They can be reworked in many different ways and in many different cultural communities.

A Skye Plantation illustrates a natural science curriculum grounded, so to speak, in the child's own environment. Any environment can be used for this purpose, from a farm to the seashores to a vacant lot in the heart of a city. Issues involving sociological and political influences on science will arise in each context.

Shadows and ThinkerTools illustrate principles that need to be addressed in any physical science curriculum. In particular, the fact that students bring an array of complex intuitive beliefs *to* such courses must be taken account of. Children construct their own informal explanations of the physical world—climate, gravity, electricity, and the like. Every living human is naturally disposed to try to make sense of the environment, and to predict it. The curriculum should start from that point.

Nautical Studies illustrates a type of specialized secondary school that could be much more prevalent than it is. There are relatively few high schools for performing arts or for science and technology. An important distinction must be made between high schools that are apprenticing students for real adult occupations, and so-called vocational high schools that may be attended primarily by students of low ability. Students at all levels of ability ought to be enabled to work together—as they will in real life—to prepare for various occupations within fields such as marine studies, architecture, or commercial art.

6/ Basic Skills

The curriculums I have described incorporate a number of literacy and numeracy mechanics. In the Neighborhood Explorer these included counting, writing down numbers, reading street signs, and writing down the names of neighbors. In Shadows, children measured the distance of a light from an object, wrote Fooler Recipes, and read each other's experimental reports. These mechanics, which are common to all projects, are what is meant here by the term *basic skills*.

Basic skills may be divided into two groups. First-order skills are those that deal with relatively small units of skill, such as learning letter-sound correspondences, reading words, writing words, and adding numbers. Second-order skills are those that deal with larger units, such as predicting what a story will be about, planning the structure of a paragraph, or deciding whether an arithmetic answer makes sense.

First- and second-order skills are clearly interrelated, and they should be taught together. Most important, the connections between basic skills and projects such as the Neighborhood Explorer should be made immediately and strongly.

Reading, writing, and arithmetic arose as tools of the trade. They were invented to deal with commodities, to keep track of who sold what to whom in the Phoenician trading ports, and to send messages about business matters. Instruction in the use of these tools always used to be in the form of apprenticeships. Instruction was embedded in practical enterprises that had important consequences.[1]

Over the next few thousand years, reading, writing, and arithmetic became reified as ends in themselves. Instruction was disconnected from real-world objectives. Schools lost sight of the fact that a tool isn't important—indeed, it is scarcely even defined—unless it is needed for something. To construct an effective basic skills program, instruction must be put back into meaningful contexts.

This is done in two ways: first, children should use their first- and second-order basic skills immediately in projects such as the Neighborhood Explorer and Shadows. The teacher need not wait until students have learned how to spell perfectly, for example, before encouraging them to write down the results of an experiment. This is particularly true because the application process itself needs to be practiced as early as possible. Decisions have to be made: what is the main point of my science report? What numbers should be added together? Learning to make these decisions is as important as learning to spell and calculate.

This tactic is an application of the exploratory principle of apprenticeship. It is through exploratory efforts that children learn how to adapt their basic skills, tune them to fit new settings, and gain the courage to attempt variations. Eventually, prowess in basic skills will catch up with the child's interests and imagination. Putting basic skills to use in the meantime, imperfect though they may be, helps children to understand why the basics are being learned and why they are so important.

A second means of maintaining connections between skills and projects is to use materials from projects in basic skills lessons. Spelling, for example, can be practiced on words gleaned from neighborhood exploration or on scientific words from shadow experiments.

THE IMPORTANCE OF PRACTICE

Ballet dancers work out at the *barre* every morning without fail, no matter how professionally expert they have become, tennis champions still practice with trainers, and chess experts continue to play matches with their seconds. The objective of all this practice is not merely to keep physical (or mental) muscles from going flabby but to accomplish what psychologists call *overlearning*—practice that goes beyond criterion, beyond the level of expertise that represented the initial objective. Practice beyond this level is what produces automaticity—the ability to conduct a routine without thinking about it consciously. Automaticity frees the mind to deal with new information.[2]

Car drivers have a lot to look out for: oncoming traffic, the child playing ball near the curb, the baby in the back seat, traffic signals, route signs. Steering, pedaling, braking, and estimating the car's distance from the curb must become automatic in order for drivers to have "room" in their working memories for dealing with unexpected events, such as the child who darts out into the street.

Similarly, reading, writing, and arithmetic incorporate routines that must become automatic if room is to be available in the student's working memory for puzzling about the kind of questions that arise in curriculums like the Desperate Journey (and throughout life). A student may reflect, for example, "The more food the

Murrays carry, the slower they will have to go, and the more food they'll need . . ."—and unconsciously draw on a number of basic skills. These skills must be over-learned, practiced well beyond a criterion level, to become automatic. It is imperative to embed basic skills training in projects that fascinate children so that we can keep them practicing, practicing, practicing.

READING AND WRITING

The origins of integrated language arts instruction can be traced to the ancient Greeks, but it was the Romans who devised a method that could be applied on a mass scale. This school of pedagogy was summarized in *Institution Oratoria* (A.D. 95), by Marcus Fabius Quintilianus. At the heart of the approach was the belief that linguistic ability (Quintilianus called it *facilitas*) was a single, unitary human capacity, whether it was employed in listening, speaking, reading, or writing. Quintilianus explained that sight, sound, and sense were to be constantly interrelated, and both prose and poetry were to be used, to provide variety.[3]

Students first listened as the instructor read or spoke. The pupils spoke in response, and then wrote—sometimes imitating the form or style of what they heard or read, sometimes creating versions of their own—and finally read aloud what they had written. They also read the work of others, of course. The materials were initially simple, like Aesop's fables, but systematically increased in complexity until they included advanced subject matter and the full roster of disciplines that college students study today—literature, history, science, and so on. A modern version of the Quintilianus system, at the advanced level, is called the "writing across the curriculum" (WAC) movement.[4] On the elementary level, it is currently known as the "whole language approach" to literacy instruction.[5]

Comprehension and composition. In the case of literacy, second-order skills are often collected under the rubrics *comprehension* (in reading) and *composition* (in writing).

Second-order skill training should not wait upon first-order skill mastery, and a good way to conduct second-order literacy skill training is to follow exactly the strategy that Quintilianus recommended: read aloud to children, and talk about what was read. The second-order skills to be developed during this exercise are those of active listening, which will later be transferred to active reading.

Active listening and reading involve a small set of basic strategies that will be reiterated and eventually reflected upon and articulated. They include monitoring one's own comprehension, making connections, and making predictions.[6] The teacher models these processes and elicits them from the children.[7]

Suppose, for example, the teacher reads aloud this passage from the *The Desperate Journey:*

> The next morning, after breakfast of oatmeal porridge, the family made ready. Their goods were lashed securely on to the cart and Davie brought the goatskin bag of money dripping from the burn.

Here the teacher might think aloud: "From the burn? Let me check my memory. What was the money doing in the burn?" The children see that she is checking her understanding and is connecting a phrase she has just read to her prior knowledge. To answer, which the children are eager to do, they will have to follow suit. The reading continues:

"Are you ready, Kate?" James asked quietly. "Aye, James." She looked at the blackened walls of what had been her clean, bright home. "Farewell, Culmailie. We may never see you again." Kirsty began to weep a little, and Davie put a hand out to comfort her. "Don't look back, Kirsty. It is better to look forward."[8]

"Oh dear," the teacher says, "that makes me think of a time when I had to leave something behind, and go on to something new. It was when I was eight years old, and we moved to a new town. I remember how sad I was about leaving my friends, and leaving the special places that we used to play. Do you remember any times like that?" The children learn to articulate how literature connects with feelings and personal memories. They might also go on to discuss the meaning of what it means to look forward rather than to look back.

There are many ways in which writing exercises can grow out of such a discussion. Children can rewrite in their own words what has been read to them. The ability to paraphrase and summarize is an important second-order skill, as Quintilianus well knew. The children might also write about their own memories of leaving something behind or about a time when they discovered that it was better to look to the future than to look back at the past.

As in the case of listening and reading, there are strategies that expert writers use that can be usefully applied in writing exercises. An important guide in writing instruction is Donald Graves, whose approach applies many principles of apprenticeship. He suggests that teachers, using an overhead projector or a large tablet, always write with the children, in order to allow them to follow the teacher's own composition processes, which she vocalizes as she goes along. Graves frequently uses the term *studio* to indicate the atmosphere of shared productivity that he wants teachers to create in the classroom. The strategies that Graves leads children to develop include generating ideas (a process that will have been assisted by active listening), talking to oneself and others about one's writing (conferencing), revising, editing, and publishing.[9]

Revising is an especially difficult and complex second-order skill, one for which scaffolding is often needed.[10] Two specialists in the psychology of writing, Marlene Scardamalia and Carl Bereiter, have conducted a number of investigations into the types of advice, or prompts, that can help children learn how to revise. In one study, children were given slips of paper on which the appropriate prompt was written: "People won't see why this is important," "People will be interested in this part," "This doesn't sound quite right," "I'd better give an example." The teacher modeled the use of such prompts, and the children both modeled and applied them. It was important that the children remained free to decide which of the prompts they wanted to use. The skill to be developed was deciding when revision was necessary. If the decision is always made by the teacher, then the child's own self-guiding skills will never develop.[11]

Enciphering and deciphering. In terms of first-order skills, literacy most fundamentally involves the fact that we have developed a written code to represent speech. When we read, we decipher that code. When we spell, we encipher our speech. There are, of course, many kinds of ciphers—whole-word ciphers, for instance. But the cipher in most common use today involves the alphabetic principle, wherein a letter, or a set of letters, represents a phoneme—a small unit of speech. We mix and match phonemes to produce spoken words, and we mix and match the letters that represent phonemes to produce written words. This principle was formulated by the Greeks from various conventions for marking vowel and consonant sounds that had previously been used, rather inconsistently, by various Oriental cultures, including Egyptian and Persian.

> Generally speaking, we write consonants and vowels in the same way as the ancient Greeks did . . . Vowels are expressed by special signs on equal footing with consonants, as in the writing of the syllable *ta* by means of the signs *t* plus *a*. This . . . is characteristic of all the Western writings no matter how much they may differ in outer form: Greek, Latin, runic, Slavonics, Morse, etc.[12]

The signs and combinatorial principles for writing down speech therefore constitute a major knowledge base that all literate individuals must acquire. This is sometimes referred to in cognitive circles as the *orthographic cipher*. In commercial reading programs, it is labeled *phonics*, a catch-all term that refers in part to orthographic rules and in part to teaching methods.[13]

The orthographic cipher is common to both reading and spelling, but this connection is seldom made. Children are typically taught the cipher in reading lessons. They learn to "sound out" words. In spelling lessons, they usually memorize lists of words. Only occasionally are spelling rules taught, and they are almost never related to reading rules. We need to show children that the same cipher is involved in both reading and spelling. The rules they learn in one case need to be systematically related to the rules they learn in the other. Only then will they acquire an interconnected body of knowledge about how the alphabetic principle works.

An ingenious way of doing this was developed in the 1920s by Romalda Spalding. She adapted and extended a system developed by Samuel Orton, a neurologist who had a special interest in reading disabilities (dyslexia). Adding many techniques of her own to Orton's principles, Spalding developed a method for teaching reading to normal children.[14]

Phonograms. A Spalding teacher begins by teaching a set of phonograms—basic letter-sound units, such as the "tuh" sound that the letter *t* makes and the two sounds "eh, ee" (written /ĕ/ and /ē/) that the letter *e* makes.[15]

The first fifteen or twenty minutes of each lesson are taken up with learning new phonograms and reviewing old ones. The teacher always begins by modeling the response expected from the student. She holds up the card and says the sound or sounds that the letter(s) represent. All the sounds of a given letter are taught at once, in order of their frequency. This helps connect a set of sounds to a single graphic pattern, so that students don't, in effect, set up separate mental addresses for the /ă/ in apple, the /ā/ in ape, and so on. Students are thus prepared for the strategy of testing several different sounds, beginning with the most frequent one, whenever they see a letter. Teaching all the sounds at once also sets up intonation patterns that help students to remember them. A class may practice by reciting phonograms in unison.

The connections between the sight of a letter and the phonemes it represents are established through these "see-say" drills, just as basic ballet movements are established through daily practice at the *barre*. Connections are also established between the sound of a phoneme and the production of a letter: "hear-write" drills. The students produce column after column of written phonograms, and they correct their own work;

no grades are given. Phonograms are taught in sets small enough (usually not more than four a day) that students maintain a rate of about 90 percent correct.

A word here about motivation. What I have just described may sound quite dull, but in fact it is not. It's actually fun, and it provides students with a sense of immediate accomplishment and success. In the case of students with a history of reading failure, phonogram practice does wonders for battered morales.

Within a few days, students are skilled enough to pair off and take turns being the teacher. The real teacher then circulates and takes the opportunity, as appropriate, to explain how her mind is working when she comes up against a troublesome phonogram. The other students are encouraged to follow suit, and a reflective, problem-solving environment is established. This is extended and deepened when spelling instruction begins.

Spelling. As soon as sufficient phonograms have been learned, practice in spelling begins. Explicit spelling strategies are taught. The teacher dictates a word, and the student's first job is to break it into syllables. The teacher then asks: "What's the first sound you say?" This will be a phonogram that has previously been drilled. The form of the question is important. "What's the first sound you say?" rather than "What letter does it begin with?" sets up a clear procedural step: first, the students should reflect on what they have heard. Then the next instruction is given: "Now, write it." Again and again the students implement this strict procedure: "What's the first [or next] sound you say? Now, write it." As with phonograms, students take turns being the teacher, and the real teacher guides reflection and articulation in a problem-solving atmosphere.

Particular words in the spelling lessons can be assembled from any source. Spalding uses a list of 1,700 words compiled in order of frequency. Words can also be collected from the context in which a basic skills program is embedded—for example, from the book *The Desperate Journey*, from a social studies curriculum, or, in adult literacy programs, from the workplace.

Spelling rules. In the course of spelling, problems soon arise. In fact, the first word on the Spalding list, *me*, generates a problem, because students must determine which of its two sounds the *e* will take. Fortunately, there is a simple rule to help them decide: a vowel usually takes its long sound if it occurs at the end of a syllable. The rule doesn't guarantee accuracy, but it increases the likelihood of being correct and in this case it solves the *me* problem. The rule can be tested when the fourth word on the list, *go*, is encountered, and it works again. Between twenty and thirty rules, gradually increasing in complexity and diversity, are eventually taught.

The bridge from spelling to reading. Spalding's most remarkable contribution is her invention of a marking system that enables children to connect spelling rules to reading. The system consists of five simple conventions, including the following: when two or more letters represent a single phoneme (as *sh* does, for example), that phonogram is underlined. When a phonogram has more than one sound, and is not taking its first (most frequent) sound, then a little number is written above it—the number of the sound it takes. Given a silent *e*, for which there can be five possible reasons, a subscript indexing the rule in question is attached to the letter. Double lines are used to mark uncommon sounds.

In the case of *already* in Figure 7, the numeral 3 above

pro vi si̲on

(si with 2 above)

ac co̲rd in̲g

ål re̲åd y

(ål with 3 above, rea with 2 above)

7. Three words marked by the
Spalding code.

the *a* indicates that the letter is taking its third most frequent sound. The phonogram *ea* has been underlined (because it is a single sound, not composed of the sounds that *e* and *a* represent separately), and a 2 has been placed above *ea* to show that the phonogram takes its second most frequent sound in this case.

Using these conventions, students learn to mark the words they have spelled, in an atmosphere of problem solving. First the words are separated into syllables, and then the syllables are marked. Each student takes a turn explaining how a word is to be marked and justifies each marking by reference to the appropriate rule. Any marking will be accepted, provided the student can justify it. The teacher marks the word on the blackboard, and the children write and mark it in notebooks, which eventually become personal glossaries filled with hundreds of marked words.

This approach recalls the reflection principle of the apprenticeship model. After spelling a word, the student reflects upon it and abstracts both its components and the rules they embody. The marking system itself highlights these components and rules in roughly the same way that a football coach highlights the parts of a play by drawing lines electronically on a videotape.

The marking system is the bridge that connects spelling to reading. After a few hours of practice children find themselves spontaneously marking, mentally, words they see on street signs, buildings, and so on. They "see" these words in their marked form. They are developing, in effect, a coded sight vocabulary. They are not merely recognizing words by sight but are, at the same time, recognizing what parts of them embody generalizable rules. This ability is a great improvement over the simple acquisition of a list of sight words, because it provides the student with guidelines for reading by analogy.

All of the analytical work and rule acquisition is done within the context of spelling. This is different from the "sounding out" instructional procedures that most reading programs use. It has been argued that "sounding out" interrupts the natural flow of the reading process, because it trains students to deal sequentially and slowly with words they might otherwise be able to process as wholes at a glance. But spelling is already a sequential, slow procedure. A word cannot be written down all at once; it must be dealt with one part at a time. Using spelling to teach the signs and combinatorial principles for writing down speech thus does not interrupt the natural flow of spelling. On the contrary, it expedites it, by providing rules for deciding between alternatives. Once they become automatic, the rules operate very quickly.[16]

Reading. In the Spalding system, reading is never taught as such. Children read the words they spell, of course. Daily, they read and reread lists and lists of words. Then, on a very special day in the lives of the younger children, reading in real books begins. The children have in fact learned how to read, and they can now pick up (simple) books and read. Emphasis is always upon the classics, great books written for children by authors who loved words and who were not reluctant to present children with words they might not immediately know. Teacher and child will eventually tackle the problem of deciding how new words are to be marked and pronounced. A story is never interrupted for that purpose, however. If a word is difficult, the teacher pronounces it and quickly puts up its marked form on the blackboard. Because the marking code has been highly practiced, the child can see at a glance how the word should be pronounced. The teacher doesn't have to interrupt the flow of ideas to "sound it out." Often just the first step in marking, dividing the word into syllables, does the trick. The reading lesson itself focuses upon meaning and enjoyment, and upon comprehension training—the second-order skills previously described.

From literacy to arithmetic. We have examined the process through which this training program in first-order literacy skills explicitly teaches the alphabetic principle (orthographic cipher), builds and clarifies connections between reading (deciphering) and spelling (enciphering), and provides a set of analytical strategies for dealing with new words. One of the most important aspects of this program is its emphasis upon problem solving. I have seen a number of cases, interestingly, in which children's arithmetic skills improved following a few months of training in this literacy program. I believe this is because the children transferred the analytical, problem-solving strategies they were learning in their reading classes to their arithmetic assignments. They were learning to pay close attention to details, and they were learning that rules and strategies can be invoked to deal with new problems. When they applied those same principles to arithmetic, improvement was sometimes dramatic.

ARITHMETIC

As in the case of literacy, basic numeracy skills can also be classified as first-order and second-order procedures. The first-order procedures include learning and retrieving "number facts" and calculating. These skills are analogous to those of learning and retrieving phonograms, spelling, and marking words. The second-order arithmetic procedures are analogous to those of comprehension and composition—except that in mathematical circles, they are usually collected under the rubric *problem solving*.

Problem-solving strategies. The second-order procedures involved in mathematical thinking may be understood as a series of questions the student must learn to ask.

To *monitor comprehension,* for example, a student asks, Do I understand this term? This equation? This operation? Can I put it in my own words? Can I explain what I'm doing, and why? Is this logical? To *make connections,* a student asks, Do I know another problem like this? A procedure that worked before? Does this remind me of something? If I make a list of every statement in this problem, what connections can I discover? To *make predictions,* a student asks, Can I guess how this is going to come out? If I do this operation first, what should be done second? Do I need to carry out this operation? And to *reformat,* a student asks, Can I draw a picture of the problem? A diagram? Can I put it into symbols? Can I put it into words?

In the problem-solving literature, procedures of this type are called heuristics, or rules-of-thumb. They are more flexible and exploratory than algorithms, step-by-step "recipes" for producing answers.[17] It is important for children to acquire heuristics from the beginning of instruction in mathematics, long before they have become skilled in first-order calculation routines. Second-order skill training is initiated through stories, puzzles, and games.

Two games illustrate how a foundation of mathematical concepts and heuristics may be built in the minds of young children. These games are recommended by Michael Holt and Zoltan Dienes, designers of mathematics pedagogy and materials.[18]

The Rainbow Toy game involves coloring. The teacher or parent first cuts a square out of white cardboard, and paints each corner a different color (see Figure 8). Four colors are used, and the front and back of each corner are painted the same color. This cardboard square is placed in the middle of a large sheet of paper that has a different drawing or word—*roof, wall, window,* or *door*—on each edge. The children, meanwhile, are given a stack of uncolored house drawings, with which to play the game. The cardboard square is rotated on the paper so that the square's colored corners point at the words or drawings, and the children color their drawings accordingly.

If we imagine four colors for the patterned corners in Figure 8a and follow the sequence there, in the first house the roof will be gray, the walls black, the window pink, and the door red. Now the square is rotated one step. In the next house the roof will be red, the walls gray, the window black, and the door pink. Eventually the children have colored four houses, and the square is flipped over. Will the houses now be different? Most

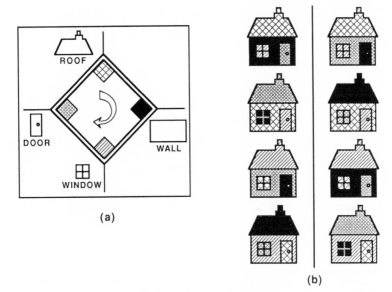

(a)

(b)

8. The Rainbow Toy game.

children predict they will not be, and they are eager to prove their prediction by coloring a new set of houses (see Figure 8b).

In the Square Dance game, four children hold hands, facing inward, to make a square—two boys, Earl and Sam, are facing each other, separated by two girls, Liz and Betty. Earl and Sam are asked to change places without letting go of their neighbors' hands. Liz and Betty must not let go of their neighbors' hands either, and they must stay where they are, though they may swivel around like tops on the same spot. At the end of the dance, no arms must be crossed. After a glorious tangle, the children will end up facing outward. Then they must return to their starting positions.

The two games have the same underlying mathematical pattern. Holt and Dienes urge that the children not be told of the pattern, however, and that they instead be encouraged to make such discoveries for themselves. One game involves primarily visual and imaging processes, the other motor processes. Quite literally, the games are building neurological analogs—different brain representations of the same mathematical concepts. Later, these representations will be interfaced with formal symbols and rules of geometry.

Computation and calculation. The first-order skills of adding, subtracting, multiplying, and dividing should be taught together, and they should be taught using concrete materials. Good teachers have always known this, and many curriculums (Montessori's, for example) can be cited in illustration. Support for these principles can also be found in the research literature and, perhaps, in the outstanding mathematical capabilities of Japanese children, who are instructed not only by means of the abacus but also by means of tiles (see Figure 9).[19] The Japanese tiles, cut out of cardboard, are used much like Unifix Cubes, which are made out of plastic and were presumably inspired by the wooden cubes in the structural arithmetic program developed by Catherine Stern and her colleagues.[20] These are all good pedagogical systems.

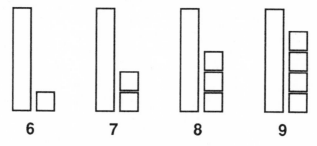

6   7   8   9

9. Tiles representing numbers.

These materials, though concrete, *encode* numbers, just as words and written numerals do. There is a strict, rule-based relationship between a concrete unit and a number unit. The use of a concrete code enables a child to learn to represent logical mathematical relationships as images and motor movements and as words and written signs. It is, however, as with spelling and reading, very important to make sure these mutually enriching symbologies are strongly interconnected.

I know of one curriculum that provides truly adequate drill and practice in interconnecting spoken, written, and concrete (visual-motor) representations of arithmetic facts and procedures. It was written by John C. Gray, who was, in 1910, superintendent of schools in Chicopee, Massachusetts. His book on his method was entitled *Number by Development*, and the term *development* referred to the growth of the idea of number in the child's mind. The book, roughly half of which I will survey here, covers about three years of instruction, from counting through fractions.[21]

Gray's method was based on Dewey's theory. In 1895 Dewey had published *The Psychology of Number* in collaboration with James McLellan, principal of the Ontario School of Pedagogy in Toronto.[22] Their book contains interesting and practical ideas about the origin of number concepts in children and the best methods of developing these concepts into mature mathematical forms. The connections between counting, adding, multiplying, subtracting, and dividing are emphasized. Dewey called the procedural interconnections "parting and wholing":

> The emphasis is all the time upon the performance of certain mental processes; the product, the particular fact or item of information to be grasped, is simply the outcome of this process. There is a given whole to be counted off into minor wholes; a group of objects to be

marked off into subgroups . . . Then the number of subgroups, minor unities or parts has to be counted up in
order to find the numberical value of the original whole.
The entire interest is in the actual process of distinguish-
ing the whole into its parts, and combining the parts to
as to make up the value of the whole.[23]

Counting and addition. Gray's curriculum initially
suggests that the teacher take a group of children to a
worktable supplied with sticks, cubes or other similar
objects. Assuming the children can count at least to
three, the teacher says: "Show me two blocks." The
children each collect two blocks. "Show me another
two." They do. "Show me another two." They do.
"Now, how many twos do you have?" The children
answer: "Three twos." "Count them," the teacher says,
and the children do. Then the teacher asks again: "How
many twos?" and the children again answer, "Three
twos."

At this point the teacher says: "Now, this is the way
the crayon [or pencil or the chalk] says 'Three twos,' "
and she writes "3 2's." She explains that this is the
"short way" the crayon says it. There is also a "long
way": she writes "2 + 2 + 2."

She will work through other variations, using sums
up to twenty, and having the children show her how
the crayon "says it." She will then ask them to read it
the "long way" ("a four and a four and a four," for
example), and to say it the "long way" with the crayon
(the children write "4 + 4 + 4").

The teacher also constructs groups of objects and the
children say or write them. The teacher's groups may,
of course, be quite challenging. Sometimes children
practice reading "what the chalk has said," by saying
aloud "three and three and three" or "three threes,"

depending on what is written on the blackboard. Sometime they transcribe groups that have been drawn on the blackboard. They also "take dictation," constructing, at their desks, groups of objects (see Figure 10). The teacher then erases the blackboard, and the children write out the whole exercise from the groups on their desks.

These variations are practiced for about two months.

THE LANGUAGE OF + AND 'S   67

The dictations will accumulate into a form as follows:

$3+4$	$4+2$
4 2's	$2+4$
2 4's	$4+4+4$
$1+3$	$3+2$
3 3's	4 1's
$3+3$	$1+4$
$4+3$	2 2's

The constructions on the pupil's desk should be in corresponding form when completed, as follows:

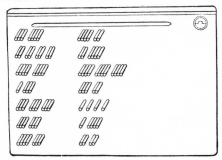

NOTE.—If pupils are trained to make these constructions on the left half of their desks, it will leave the right half clear for them to use in the written work which follows. See (c).

10. Concrete and written language of addition.

The children are often required to vocalize softly to themselves. Gradually they build strong, automatic connections between the imagery of the materials, words, written numerical symbols, and number concepts.

Multiplication. In introducing the concept of multiplication, all that happens at first is that the teacher tells the child, "Another way the crayon can say four threes is 4 × 3." Exercises continue as before, but now the children use two "short ways" and sometimes have the option of choosing the one they prefer.

A new type of exercise is introduced: The teacher writes "4 +" on the blackboard, and says, "I want you to make this. It means four and anything else that you wish." Then the teacher writes "× 3" and says, "This means as many threes as you please. How many are you going to make?" She lists on the blackboard possible elements like those in Figure 11, and the children make optional constructions of objects at their desks, samples of which are shown in the lower part of Figure 11.

Simple equations. When they begin to learn about equations, the children are introduced to the equals sign and are taught to say "will make" when they see it. If they see "6 =", they take six objects and construct a group expression with them: 4 + 2, 2 + 4, 2 × 3, 3 + 3, or anything else they choose. Then the full expression is written: 6 = 4 + 2, for example. This is called "making a number story," and practice goes on for about three weeks in progressively more complex forms.

Subtraction. In learning subtraction, the students begin with their pile of sticks or other objects and listen to the teacher's instructions. "Let us all take six," she (*a*) Blackboard Dictation.

5 +	+ 6
3 ×	6 +
× 4	3 's
3's	2 ×
+ 6	× 4
× 5	6's
5 +	4 ×

(*b*) Pupils' Seat Work.

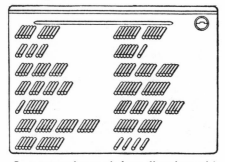

In construction work from dictations without choice it is evident that the concrete work would be the same on all the desks, the written work alone showing variations. In construction work from these elliptical dictations, however, there may be as many va-

11. Concrete and written language of multiplication.

says. Next, "let us all take away two." Having done this, she asks, "How many are left?" She then writes on the blackboard, saying as she does so, "This is the way the crayon says it: 6 − 2 = 4."

The teacher continues to talk as she writes, and the children follow her example, talking softly as they rearrange their sticks. The children are next taught a new way of using their sticks: they turn the set that is "taken away" sideways, as in Figure 12. Place value will eventually be taught by means of bundles of ten sticks and bundles (in principle) of a hundred sticks. The child can then see that thirteen is composed of one bundle of ten, and three single sticks. Unifix and other structural arithmetic programs, such as those of Dienes and Montessori, use a similar method: place values are taught in concrete terms before children learn written "borrow-

"TAKE AWAY"   101

(b) Seat Construction.

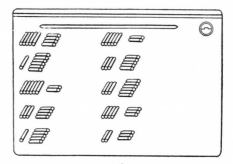

(c) Seat Written Work.

9 − 4 = 5	7 − 2 = 5
7 − 6 = 1	8 − 5 = 3
8 − 2 = 6	9 − 6 = 3
7 − 4 = 3	7 − 3 = 4
6 − 5 = 1	5 − 3 = 2

NOTE.—In a "take away" exercise like this the dictation should be erased before the child begins to write from his construction work. After a few exercises in "take away" like the above the teacher should cease giving exercises consisting wholly of subtraction expressions. The dictations should be "take away" and "will make" mixed.

(d) Blackboard Dictation—Mixed.

12. Concrete and written language of subtraction.

ing" notation. This is the only way to make sure the underlying logic of the written notation is fully understood.

Division. Learning division involves a similar set of directions by the teacher, which the students also carry out with sticks at their desks: "Take eight," she says. "Make it into fours." Next, she asks, "How many fours?" After the children have answered, she asks them to "take six." She tells them, "You may find how many twos it has." Writing on the blackboard as she talks, she continues:

"This is how the crayon tells us to take six and find out how many twos it has: $6 \div 2$." As the teacher goes from the top dot to the lower in writing the sign for division, she says, "Has–how–many . . ." She next says, "Now I will make the crayon tell the whole story," and she writes "$6 \div 2 = 3$."

The notion of "bundles" is now introduced, and the children become able to deal with "$8 \div 3$" and other such shockers, which Gray has the teacher introduce without warning: "How many whole bundles are there?" she asks. "Are there any left over toward another bundle? How many?" She then tells the children, "You may place your part bundle beside your whole bundles. Here is how the crayon tells the whole story: $8 \div 3 = 2\frac{2}{3}$. Eight has-how-many threes? It has two, and two left over toward making another bundle of three." Variations on all of this go on for another month.

CONTROVERSIES AND SOLUTIONS

Controversies arise, again and again, over teaching basic skills.[24] Some argue that basic skills should be taught in practical, meaningful terms, such as making change or reading street signs; others say that it is the higher-order problem-solving skills that should be taught, and that the practical applications can be figured out as needed; and still others assert that lower-order mechanics such as calculation and phonics are the heart of "the basics," and higher-order skills, such as problem solving, should be taught in other subjects—social studies, for example. For hundreds of years, arguments over how to teach basic skills have bounced back and forth among these three positions. Each has advocates who (sometimes fanatically) argue against the other two.

The controversies serve the important function of sharpening our awareness of various issues. It has never made any theoretical sense, however, to emphasize one camp to the exclusion of the other two. Good basic skills programs in reading, writing, and arithmetic should integrate all three positions: training should be embedded in rich, meaningful contexts; and it should emphasize the development and automatization of *both* first-order and second-order skills, which children should be encouraged to apply in context, as best they can, from the first day of instruction.

7 / Making the Best of Things

Ideal, or closer to ideal, instructional environments are increasing in number, but they are not yet plentiful. How do we cope, in the meantime, with what is?

The starting point is to recognize that schools are presently organized in ways that make certain problems—for teachers, children, and parents—inevitable. There are three interlocking wellsprings of trouble: fractionated curriculums, grouping regulations, and test-driven planning. These wellsprings are protected by long-standing policies and laws. Making the best of things, the topic of this chapter, refers to ways of operating within the existing mandates. Making things better, the topic of the next chapter, refers to ways of sidestepping the mandates themselves.

THE FRACTIONATED CURRICULUM

School programs are fractionated, a problem that stems in part from Thorndike's efforts to turn education into a series of "countable" scientific enterprises. Every aspect of a program is broken down into something that can be counted. Days are subdivided into periods, periods are subdivided into lessons, lessons are subdivided into objectives (for example, working ten

145

problems correctly). Even within a forty-minute period devoted to the same subject matter (social studies, for example), there is often no clear unifying theme. There are exercises to be gone through, daily lesson "scripts" that the children have learned to expect, but there is little internal organization to the material. At the end of the period, work in one area is "put away," and work for the next area is "gotten out." Sometimes students go to another room and another teacher. The adjacent lessons seldom have any connection and the lessons that address the topic just covered, won't come around again for at least a day, and sometimes not for several days or even a week.

It is now known that fractionated programs make it almost impossible for children to acquire and retain information. Fractionated instruction maximizes forgetting, inattention, and passivity. Both children and adults acquire knowledge from active participation in holistic, complex, meaningful environments organized around long-term goals. Today's school programs could hardly have been better designed to prevent a child's natural learning system from operating.

I have worked with many parents who are concerned about their child's memory and attention problems. A tiny percentage of these children have bona-fide learning disabilities. The vast majority are simply struggling with the problem of having to remember massive amounts of disconnected material, day in and day out. The material often makes little sense in itself and bears little relationship to meaningful long-term objectives in a child's world. These same children can give you reams of baseball statistics, science-fiction details, or information about any area they are interested in and have been able to investigate. They display excellent memories and capacities for concentration. Sometimes, on intelligence tests and on standardized achievement tests, their scores are way above average—they know more, and solve problems better, than perhaps 98 percent of the children their age. They are well behaved in school, they do their work, but they get C's, D's, and F's on homework and tests. They are up against the hopeless task of trying to remember endless streams of disconnected information. For bright children the task can seem so trivial and boring that they won't even try.

Let me emphasize that this is not the fault of teachers. In most school districts, the curriculum and the organization of the school day have been prescribed by school committees, supervisors, and in some cases by state legislatures. The material that has to be learned will appear on prescribed year-end tests that the teacher must administer—and if the children haven't learned it, they won't be promoted. Teachers are as concerned over this as parents are. And teachers, like children, are exhausted by the relentless pressure of the fractionated school day.

For those faced with this reality, the only solution is to teach strategies for dealing with fractionated learning situations. A major source of failure at the advanced elementary level, for example, is the vocabulary requirement. Children must memorize dictionary definitions of perhaps a dozen unrelated words at a time. They are tested on these words at least once a week, sometimes cumulatively.

Scientists who study the natural growth of vocabulary knowledge have demonstrated unequivocally that word meanings are never learned in this way in normal circumstances.[1] Word meanings are learned from repeated use and from context—from extensive conversation and reading. The meaning of a word is something like a location in a network—a pointer to a web of interconnected implications. Meaning is built; it must be constructed from other meanings that an individual already has. Vocabulary knowledge will not come into existence through memorizing dictionary definitions any more than nourished bodies will come into existence through memorizing recipes.

Nevertheless, if children are required to memorize dictionary definitions, they can be taught mnemonic tricks—a bizarre image, for example, that connects a word to a meaning—that will enable them to pass their vocabulary tests.[2] This solves the immediate problem, but it has nothing to do with intellectual growth, of course, which is the purpose of the vocabulary requirement.

Mnemonic tricks, however, illustrate the principle of making connections. In this case, they are artificial connections that serve the temporary purpose of keeping information in mind long enough to reproduce it on a test. But to build long-term knowledge, a child needs to make meaningful, purposeful connections. Parents and teachers can help children do this, even when dealing with fractionated curriculums, by following the lead of the programs described in Chapter 4. Books and lessons can be extended and elaborated. Each assignment, each topic, can be a starting point, not an ending point. Which aspects of the topic will be especially meaningful to the child? What are her talents? What will he spend a long time doing? A child's interests can be used as a magnet, a focal point for interrelating information from other books, from museums, from educational television, from visits with others (including some experts, if possible) who have the same enthusiasm for the subject. Parents and teachers can work with each other to find connecting principles and organizing themes. These themes can be anchored to active, long-term projects—making a collage, putting on a play, building something, mounting a fair—projects that build connections between didactic material and personal experience.

I recognize, however, that teachers may say: "I have thirty children to control. And you expect me to put on a *fair?*"

GROUPING REGULATIONS

Schooling is conducted for the most part inside stacks and rows of small containers, each confining twenty to thirty active, growing bodies. When presented with endless streams of disconnected information that has almost no relationship to matters of interest to them, these bodies (and minds) will, if they are normal, look around for something interesting to do. Whatever they come up with will almost certainly not fit in with the teacher's plans.

Losing control of a class is probably a teacher's worst fear. This fear is by no means imaginary. In September a teacher faces twenty to thirty schoolwise youngsters who will immediately set about testing her ability to control them. Knowledge of her management skills will sweep across the class, and the children will quickly make a determination about what they can and cannot get away with. The school year will begin in a mood of peace, or a mood of war.

Most of today's classrooms are not exciting apprenticeship environments keyed to the aspirations and experiences of the students who are in them. Students are brought together by law, administratively collated into groups of relative strangers, and in effect ordered to behave as if they are learning what adults have decided they ought to learn. It is extremely important to remember that this is what most people—even the students themselves—think schools ought to be.[3] It is generally considered right and proper for children to sit quietly and learn from adults—and learn also, in the process, how to behave in society, how to be polite and respectful in the presence of superiors, and how to get along in a workplace that will expect similar behavior. Schools, in other words, are designed to have a socializing influence, an aim that is often given precedence over their intellectualizing influence.[4] Most parents will tell you that though they can tolerate a teacher who does not have strong academic credentials, they cannot tolerate one who fails to teach children how to behave in the classroom.

Given this mandate, teachers have no choice but to make the development of effective crowd control procedures their number one priority. What options are available to them?

Classrooms function best with (1) clear definitions of authority and standards of expected behavior and (2) sympathetic understanding of misbehaving individuals. Teachers need to be clear and firm about such rules as:

Be polite and helpful. Listen carefully when someone is speaking. Don't fight, call names, or bother others.

Respect other people's property. Keep the room clean and neat; don't write on desks. Don't use other people's things without permission.

Don't interrupt. Wait your turn; raise your hand before you say anything, and wait until you are recognized.

Don't hit, shove, or hurt others.

Obey all school rules. These include rules about standing in line, using the library, and being on time.

Teachers are widely advised to post such rules the first day of class, and make plain from the beginning what the penalties will be for disobeying them. One disciplinary approach has been suggested by Lee Canter, who has developed a system known as *assertive discipline*.[5] Canter urges teachers to recognize that a student is not helplessly driven to disobedience by circumstances such as a poor home environment. The student chooses to misbehave and is just as able to choose not to misbehave. Canter recommends that teachers explain exactly what the consequences of a decision to misbehave will be.

> Consistency is the key to setting limits. You must provide a negative consequence for each time a student chooses to behave inappropriately. The consequence must be included in a systematic "Discipline Plan." Here are guidelines for an effective plan.
> Maximum of five consequences:
> —First: name on board, warning.
> —Second: one check, 15 minutes after school.
> —Third: two checks, 30 minutes after school.
> —Fourth: three checks, 30 minutes after school and call parents.
> —Fifth: four checks, remove from room, goes to principal or vice principal.
> —Have "severe clause" in case student severely disrupts: i.e., student immediately goes to principal.[6]

This plan applies to all students in the classroom, and a copy is sent home to parents. At the end of each day, all names and checks are erased, but a name or a check is never erased as a reward for good behavior. In the case of severely disruptive students, Canter suggests sending the student to an isolation room or to the back of another teacher's class. Canter also suggests placing a tape recorder next to the student that can be turned on if he or she disrupts, and later played for the principal or for the student's parents.

On the positive side, Canter recommends praising, sending positive notes home, and arranging for a class to earn special rewards for good behavior. One method of keeping track is to put a marble in a jar each time a student behaves well. When enough marbles have accumulated, the class as a whole gets a treat. This encourages peers to support good behavior rather than misbehavior (which is, of course, often more entertaining).

Overall, Canter's point is that teachers (like parents) must stand up for their rights, and not let themselves be misled by the belief that children cannot help themselves because they are the victims of their level of development, poor home environments, or other adverse circumstances.

Such management principles need not exclude sympathetic understanding, however. Probably the most extensive attempt to help teachers become sympathetic classroom managers was developed by Rudolf Dreikurs, a psychiatrist who followed the teachings of Alfred Adler.[7] Dreikurs explained the foundations of his approach:

> In our culture young children have few opportunities to make useful contributions toward the welfare of the family. Adults or perhaps older siblings do whatever needs to be done and the young child finds few ways to be useful and to help. It was easier for a child growing up on a farm, where there were many necessary chores to be performed, to feel that his part of the family work was a vital contribution. Nowadays, in our more affluent and urban way of life, many children make no real contribution to the welfare of others, and those who have regular chores to perform often become easily discouraged when they compare their inept performance with the more efficient and rapid accomplishments of adults or older siblings.[8]

One might add that an even greater sense of hopelessness must arise in the hearts of children from disadvantaged environments.

Dreikurs identified four goals that drive children's misbehavior: attention-getting, power, revenge, and display of inadequacy. A troublesome child is pursuing one of the following goals:

GOAL ONE [Attention]
When the child is deprived of the opportunity to gain status through his useful contributions, he usually seeks proof of his status in class through getting attention. He has the "faulty logic" that only if people pay attention to him does he have a place in his world . . .

GOAL TWO [Power]
If parents and teachers do not employ correct methods to stop the demand for undue attention, the child becomes a power seeker. The power-seeking child wants to be the boss; he operates on the faulty logic "If you don't let me do what I want, you don't love me."

GOAL THREE [Revenge]
. . . The revenge-seeking child is so deeply discouraged that he feels that only by hurting others, as he feels hurt by them, can he find his place. He views life itself and other people as hopelessly unfair . . .

GOAL FOUR [Defeat]
A child who has tried (unsuccessful) forms of attention-getting in order to achieve the feeling of "belonging," may eventually become so deeply discouraged that he gives up all hope of significance and expects only failure and defeat. He may actually feel hopeless or he may assume this position in order to avoid any further situations which might be embarrassing or humiliating to him.[9]

Dreikurs advised teachers to identify a child's goal by examining their own reactions. If a teacher feels annoyed, this indicates that the child is in pursuit of goal one, attention. If a teacher feels threatened, this suggests that the child is pursuing goal two, power, and that a contest is going on. If a teacher feels hurt, this is a sign that the child is after goal three, revenge. If a teacher feels inadequate, this indicates that the child is determined to be defeated, goal four; nothing the teacher can do will help.

Dreikurs trained teachers to confront a misbehaving child with the goal his behavior demonstrates, discuss it with him, and work out mutually agreeable substitute goals that will provide the child with a sense of status and belonging. Dreikurs also suggested that once a week, for thirty minutes, the class as a whole discuss these matters.

> Children are extremely interested in such discussion and soon begin to ask personal and pertinent questions. They volunteer information about how they have tried to gain attention, show their power, get even, or give up in discouragement, although prior to the discussion they may not have realized what they were doing.
>
> . . . The discussion turns the class into a cohesive group. The children soon begin to feel how much they have in common. The spirit of competition becomes replaced by an atmosphere of mutual empathy and help. [10]

Although some rules and some personal counseling will be necessary in every group situation, the need for them is greatly diminished when children are engaged in long-term projects that are genuinely interesting to them. In Dreikurs's terms, such situations are arranged in a way that permits all children to make a contribution and to play important roles in a group endeavor. In Canter's terms, the consequence of choosing to misbehave—banishment from the enterprise—is sharply negative. (In contrast, being banished from a boring classroom may not be perceived by a child as negative.)

But as long as grouping regulations are driven by administrative goals rather than by learning goals, much of a teacher's time and energy must be put into making children behave themselves in fractionated settings. This is an enormous waste of both the teacher's power and the children's learning power. As an example, see Figure 13, one of the saddest documents I have ever picked up in my wanderings through classrooms. It had been duplicated and passed around to a class, and posted on a bulletin board. To the teacher, to the children, to the librarian, it was a commendable example of proper school instruction and learning. To me, it was a mournful example of lost opportunities for intellectual growth. Year after year, thousands of children never find out what the treasures of a library can mean for them, because they never get beyond learning the rules.

TEST-DRIVEN PLANNING

Teachers are required, often by state law, to prepare students to pass competency tests. Sometimes these are standardized tests; sometimes they are informal tests that a local team has put together. In any case, passing tests at a specified level is what schooling is mostly about. Much of what a curriculum does, and much of what a teacher does, is driven by questions that are going to be asked on competency tests.

Such tests are intended to control the quality of educational programs. They have been part of educational practice since the 1920s, as discussed in Chapter 1, and it is difficult for most teachers, school administrators, legislators, and parents to let go of the idea that tests are the best means available of determining how effectively

I am going to describe the library.
You are not aloud to talk out loud in
the library. Don't put your books on the
chairs because other people have to sit
down. Don't put the books on top of each
other. The books are fiction and non fiction. Whisper when you have to say
something. Your not aloud to mark on the
tables. Don't mark in the books. If your
going to take a book out write your
name on the card and give it to your
teacher. Don't put candy in the books to
hide from the teacher. Don't throw candy
in the library. Don't turn books on their
face. Use a marker. Don't leave your
gum in the books. Because books can't
chew. Don't tear pages out the book.
Don't mark on the pages. Don't scrath out
words in the books. Don't pile books on
top of each other

13. A child's concept of the library.

knowledge is being transmitted from teachers to pupils.[11] Educational quality control is, of course, essential. Testing controversies do not arise from any dispute over that fact. They arise instead over definitions of quality.

A legacy from the behaviorism of the 1920s is that almost any test that is easy to administer and easy to score (and therefore economically attractive) can be said to provide a "scientific measure" of complex mental processes. This fallacy has led to widespread use of paper-and-pencil tests.

These tests, however, can tap only declarative knowledge—not procedural, conceptual, analogical, or logical knowledge. Ways of testing complex forms of knowledge certainly exist, as every carpenter, politician, chef, swimmer, engineer, mathematician, and guitar player knows and as will be discussed in Chapter 8. Complex evaluation, however, is often expensive, controversial, and may require prolonged training of evaluators.[12] There is very little incentive for the school system to develop such tests. Simple, inexpensive, easy-to-administer paper-and-pencil tests accomplish one crucial task very effectively: they provide justification for administrative decisions.

Scores on simple tests can be used to allocate funds, to hire and fire personnel, to evaluate schools, and above all, to move millions of children from one level of a massive educational bureaucracy to another.[13] It really does not matter whether tests sample important kinds of knowledge. What matters is that the constituents of the bureaucracy—administrators, lawmakers, teachers, parent groups, and the commercial suppliers—have *agreed* that the scores on particular tests shall serve as the basis of decision making.

These tests have become the major forces behind curriculum design. If educational competency is defined in terms of declarative knowledge, then declarative knowledge ought to be imparted as directly as possible. Children therefore grow up through the school system expecting to be told exactly what they are supposed to learn for written tests, writing it down, and learning it more or less adequately. This type of instruction is convenient to fractionate and easy to dispense to groups. It all works out quite well, except, perhaps, for the human race: unfortunately, there are no simple, easy-to-administer, paper-and-pencil tests driving the decisions that adults actually have to make.

SURVIVING IN THE WORLD OF TESTS

Given the fact that throughout the years of formal schooling, survival is defined in terms of declarative knowledge rather than in terms of real-world decisions, there are three positive steps that can be taken. We can do a much better job than we are presently doing of teaching youngsters how to acquire declarative knowledge and how to pass declarative tests; we can distinguish classroom tests, which should be diagnostic, prescriptive, and supportive, from achievement tests, which should be standardized across a large school population; and we can take advantage of the predictive power of standardized tests to make constructive decisions about pupil placement.

Declarative learning strategies. At the University of Delaware several short courses, known as SkilMods, have been developed to help students acquire declarative knowledge. SkilMods are based on the text and lecture materials that students have to learn, but they are designed to teach general strategies that help students master a variety of subjects. After a survey of contemporary research, the curriculum designers settled on six kinds of skills that must be assiduously practiced to become an expert student: *comprehension monitoring*, which involves asking continuously, Did I understand that phrase? That term?; *predicting*, setting up expectations for what's coming next in the lecture or text; *connecting*, tying information to other information in one's mind or notes; *summarizing*, reducing large amounts of information to key points; *reformatting*, transforming summaries into new organizations, such as outlines or charts; and *identifying text patterns*, learning to recognize the six major text patterns used in textbooks, lectures, and test questions in the Western tradition—description, comparison and contrast, definition with examples, explanation, problem and solution, and temporal ordering.

Applying these techniques while studying automatically prepares students for examinations. A test question will ask for a definition, for a description, for a history over time; it will ask students to compare and contrast, to discuss a problem and its solution, to explain something; it will require a connection, a summary, a reformatting, a prediction, or will check comprehension. If students have been exercising these cognitive procedures throughout a grading period, they will be in fine shape for a test. Knowledge will already have been set up in mental forms that match the forms on the test.

Elementary versions of these strategies can be taught from the third grade on, and perhaps even earlier. Teachers or parents can routinely teach techniques for mastering declarative information, right along with the information itself. The keys to doing this successfully are the cognitive apprenticeship teaching methods reviewed in Chapter 3—modeling, coaching, scaffolding, fostering reflection, articulation, and exploration. Teachers or parents need to show children how they monitor their own understanding of the materials the children must master, how they make predictions and connections, and so on, and then coach as children follow suit. Children can also take turns being the teacher. This is called *reciprocal teaching* by Ann Brown and Annemarie Palinscar, who have shown that their methods remarkably enhance performance on declarative tests.[14]

Classroom grading versus achievement testing. If I could change only one facet of contemporary education, I would change the practice of dispensing grades. Grades are psychologically damaging, sometimes catastrophically so, and there is absolutely no justification for them educationally or administratively.

Children are now being graded for coloring in kindergarten. I have seen a Christmas tree, colored awkwardly by inexperienced little fingers, marked with an F, right in the middle. This is not an extreme; many parents can tell similar stories. Nor do all teachers give out grades by choice. Every teacher cringes from memories of having to dispense grades, by school rules, that devastated children.

Even when grades are good, they are damaging. Something magical and wonderful has happened and parents are overjoyed, but the child has no idea how it came about. Somehow she pleased the teacher. Seeking to please the teacher then becomes the aim of education. By high school, "psyching out the teacher" is the approved means of getting A's.

The essential problem is that grades are not a good means of evaluation. They do not carry information. As children learn, they need information of many kinds: what goals to set, what to pay attention to, what kind of knowledge to apply to a new task, what strategies to use, how to know if things are going right, what a finished product is supposed to look like, and so on. This kind of monitoring from a teacher is constructive and supportive; it points to what must be learned next. It constitutes what educational researchers call *formative* evaluation.

Formative evaluation should be the only type of evaluation that occurs in classrooms. It can easily be systematized. The teacher and the child (and sometimes the parents) set goals for a learning period. At the end of the period, everyone gets together again and decides which goals have been achieved, what still needs work, and what new objectives to set. This kind of planning gradually shifts responsibility for learning and evaluation to the student, where it belongs. Teacher, child, and parents learn how to judge complex mental achievements for what they really entail, not as simplistic matters of getting a set number of answers right. The teacher and the child are partners in learning. The teacher is a coach who provides help and encouragement. She never dispenses judgment as an end in itself, as a grade.

But then what? How do we know how much a child has really learned? Sooner or later, isn't some kind of a grade needed?

There must eventually be *summative* evaluations, assessments of how much has been learned at certain checkpoints—say, every four months. As we have just seen, such evaluations are currently declarative in form; they are paper-and-pencil tests. Given that reality, it is important to understand that some paper-and-pencil tests are better—which often means fairer—than others.

Constructing good tests is a complex and technical job. The tests that teachers make up, or tests that come with commercial curriculums, are usually not technically well constructed. They are not correctly scaled for difficulty level, for accuracy, for specific versus general knowledge, and so on. Most important, they have not been designed to be independent of particular classroom factors, so that what a child knows about the subject matter, rather than about a specific curriculum or about someone's personal teaching style, can be assessed. Summative instruments need to be developed by specialists.

Summative instruments should also be standardized. They should be administered to large samples of the school population and scaled in terms of actual scores, not in terms of absolute scores. That is, the scores that most students get (about two-thirds of the tested group) should define the average range. Everyone else's scores are placed either above or below the average range. A child's relative standing in a test population can thus be determined, and as long as a child is at least in the average range, there is nothing to worry about. The child is doing as well as almost everyone else is doing. If a child is above or below the average range, then placement decisions need to be made.

Similarly, particular classes, schools, school districts, and state school systems can be evaluated by looking at the scores of their children on these summative evaluations. If a class, school, district, or state is doing at least as well as almost everyone else is doing, that is good news.

Constructive placement. The first introduction to standardized testing for many children is in connection with their so-called readiness for kindergarten. The term was popularized by Arnold Gesell, who in 1911 established the Gesell Institute for Child Development.[15] Gesell used new technologies, including film and one-way vision screens, for observing and recording child behavior, and over the years, his institute produced meticulously documented descriptions of development during infancy and childhood. Two of Gesell's associates, Louise Bates Ames and Frances Ilg, crusaded for the application of this information to school placement. A work by Ames, *Is Your Child in the Wrong Grade?*, summarized their views: "Is your child in the wrong grade? Chances are that he may be. Research conducted at the Gesell Institute in the past ten years reveals that at least one child in three may definitely be overplaced and struggling with the work of a grade which is really beyond his ability. The figure may be even larger."[16]

The researchers developed a series of tests by giving children of different ages the same task to do or question to answer. The results were compared and standardized by chronological age. In figure drawing, for example, if a sample of three-year-olds is (individually) asked to "draw Mommy," a range of scribbles and wobbly circles with dots in them will result. It is possible to classify this set of drawings into three groups: a small collection of very poor drawings that may be more like the ones that two-year-olds produce (which the researcher will recognize from having given the same task to other age groups), a small collection of very good drawings that are more like those that four-year-olds produce, and a large collection of drawings that represent what most three-year-olds produce. With this information, a particular child can be designated as having a behavioral age of two, three, or four in terms of figure drawing, by comparing her drawing with the age-standardized collection.

The Gesell team put together a battery of such tests that could be (and still is) administered to children who were chronologically old enough to begin school. The test included writing one's name, writing numbers, copying forms (such as squares and triangles), matching and remembering forms, naming animals, and answering questions about favorite home activities. By comparing the child's responses with the age-standardized sample, the child's behavioral age could be determined, and correlated with eventual school success. Which turned out to be the best predictor of school success—chronological age or behavioral age? The answer was behavioral age. Ames reported:

> Only 37% of the children [turned out to be] fully ready for the work of kindergarten and [were] promoted to first grade the following year. Forty-three percent were questionably ready for kindergarten and definitely not ready to be promoted to first grade the following year. Twenty percent were definitely unready for kindergarten.
>
> . . . A second important finding was that unready children did not, in succeeding years, "catch up" with the ready ones. Parents and teachers alike often phrase the hopeful comment, "True, he's a little bit immature right now, but he's bound to catch up." Most unready children do not, in our experience, catch up. If growth is proceeding at an "average" rate, a child's behavior grows about a year in one year's time. But it does not as a rule grow more than a year in one year, and it would have to do that if the child were going to "catch up."
>
> . . . Our conclusion at the end of three years of research . . . was, therefore, that age alone is not an adequate basis for determining the time of school entrance, and that many children legally old enough to begin school are not old enough in their behavior to do so. Your own boy or girl may be such a child.[17]

Ames is talking in terms of schools that use standard-ized curriculums. Curriculums can be designed, of course, that are suitable for children who don't score in a particular test range. If such curriculums are not avail-able, however, parents are advised, even today, over twenty years after Ames's book was originally pub-lished, to take advantage of the predictive power of standardized tests and adjust their child's grade place-ment, particularly in deciding when the child should start kindergarten.[18]

A standardized test is an actuarial device, and it works in the same way that insurance tables work. It is a fact that people who pass certain "tests" of age, sex, medical history, economic level, and so forth will probably live to be a certain age. The prediction is based on actual counts and verified on repeated samples—from census data, for example.

In an academic situation, the questions asked are not about age, sex, and medical history but about history, arithmetic, and reading skills. The data base is not from the Census Bureau but from repeated administrations of the same test (not identical questions) to children at different grade levels. Given this data base, it is possible to determine statistically, with a good degree of preci-sion, how successful a child is likely to be at various levels of a curriculum. The prediction is not 100 per-cent certain, but it is as good as anyone knows how to make it.

It is also important to understand what a standard-ized test does *not* do: it does not reveal *why* a child is succeeding or failing, and it does not say anything about a child's chances of success anywhere else but in school. Contemporary achievement tests are designed to func-tion within a particular world—a world of fractionated curriculums, declarative learning, administratively driven grouping regulations, and classroom grading procedures of uncertain quality. A well standardized test can answer one question: where does this child belong in that particular world? The test does not provide any information about where the child might belong in other worlds, academic or otherwise. Hence, test scores should be used as a guide only to the specialized terrain of contemporary formal schooling, not as a guide to any other vistas on a child's horizon.

INTEGRATION, BALANCED GOALS, AND TEST STRATEGIES

Traditional schools *can* become more suitable for children. To begin with, all adults who are involved with children—parents, teachers, relatives—can look for ways that lessons can be integrated, so that subjects are not studied in small, fractionated bits. How much integration can be accomplished will depend upon district and state regulations, and some of the methods for gathering information about them will be discussed in Chapter 8. Second, in dealing with a class of children, teachers—with the full support of parents—can balance an emphasis upon obeying rules with an understanding of the goals that troublesome children may have set for themselves and with an appreciation of educational goals that extend beyond obedience. Third, in dealing with testing requirements, a multifold strategy is best: replace grading procedures with teacher-parent-child conferences, where individual goals are set and achievements (or achievement deficiencies) are fully explained and discussed; teach children strategies for learning declarative material, so that they will be better prepared for tests they have to take; and settle gladly for average performance on year-end standardized tests—knowing that paper-and-pencil tests measure only declarative knowledge, a very small portion of the competencies that students and teachers have actually acquired.

These remedies can all be effected within the framework of traditional educational bureaucratic structures. Some, however, will want to tackle the problem of changing that structure, or escaping from it.

8/ Making Things Better

The schools we have today are the schools that most people want. They are the schools that most teachers, parents, students, voters, legislators, policy makers, superintendents, principals, cafeteria workers, guidance counselors, school psychologists, textbook publishers, school bus drivers, and education professors think we ought to have. Everyone has some complaints, but few question the basic structure of the schooling they remember from their own childhoods.[1]

How, then, is it possible for those who do question it to make changes? In particular, how is it possible to make changes quickly enough to benefit those who are children now? The answer is simple to state but of course more difficult to implement: a few like-minded people need to gather together and produce a model, a training program (of the apprenticeship variety), and a dissemination plan.

Some percentage of the people who say they favor traditional schooling do not truly find that schooling satisfactory. But they don't want to give up what they have, because they don't know what to put in its place. A working model of an apprenticeship class can demonstrate the educational alternatives that are possible.

Another percentage of the people who see the model

may want to emulate it, and a training program and curriculum packages should be ready for them. In other words, model builders should be prepared to provide the scaffolding that emulators will need. Many innovative programs never spread because their innovators expect someone else to show other people how to duplicate them. In most cases, there isn't anyone else.

With a working model in place and a dissemination package available, programs have interesting and even surprising ways of spreading, depending upon local, state, and federal circumstances.

WILLS AND WAYS

There are three ways of producing a model learning environment: changing classrooms in an ongoing school; starting a new school; and removing children from school and educating them at home. Each approach is different, of course, but they share three major requirements.

A great deal of diversified information. Contact with many other people, experts in a variety of fields, is required, even for parents who plan to educate children at home. Myriad schooling rules, procedures, and laws, for example, are involved. It is therefore essential for any network of individuals planning a model to include people who know their way around the educational system—teachers, school administrators, and school-policy experts. In order to design a program, the group should also include experts in the fields of cognitive and developmental science, in addition to experts in curriculum design and subject matter.

Visiting classes that have been set up for gifted children, is a good way to find like-minded people. The teachers involved are often those who have sought the challenge of designing new programs. Magnet schools, performing arts or science schools, and creative arts after-school programs are other places where innovative people may have set up projects or classes that they would be happy to have you observe. The innovators might also like to join your team.

Any school that looks interesting might be investigated by calling the office and asking whether a visit would be possible. If you happened to walk by Brookside School in Newark, Delaware, your attention would be caught by a dramatically exciting playground. This was built by the school and the community, including student volunteers from the University of Delaware, under the leadership of Brookside's principal, Marlene James.

Walking through the halls of Brookside, you would see that the walls are covered with children's work, including art, science reports, poems, photographs of school events, and writing of all types. The aesthetic quality of these displays is very high, and the art teacher's displays are especially stunning. The children under her tutelage (first, second, and third graders) have produced giant tropical fish in delicate and shimmering media. These hang all over the school, and several halls and doorways are decorated as underwater reefs. But the art teacher is not unique. Principal James has nurtured and drawn forth the creative potential of all her teachers, who, in turn, are drawing it forth from their pupils.

On your tour of the halls you would see some rather beamish children, hugging little books close to themselves as they walk. They have been sent to the principal's office to read to her because they are good readers or have shown impressive improvement. She receives a steady stream of children, sent by their teachers because they have done good things. "Being sent to the principal's office" means something very special here. In addition, groups of children from higher classes frequently present their projects to younger children. An apprenticeship spirit is being nurtured.

Anyone who visits a number of different schools may discover that the problems of a particular school are not representative of the district as a whole. It's important to become widely knowledgeable in this respect, and to support local innovators.

In a search for like-minded colleagues, be sure to visit the regional college of education. Get its brochures; talk to the dean. Are there innovative training programs in place? Would their originators be interested in working on a model program, or serving as consultants? Does the college have its own school or sponsor a public school that does not perpetuate the status quo? Lists of visiting speakers and public conferences at the college are another resource to broaden the horizons and extend the network of any group working to set up a model program.

A detailed plan for an apprenticeship program. Once a working group is assembled and has shared its information, its joint objective will be to design an apprenticeship learning environment that embodies the educational objectives and values held by the group. The tricky part is breaking away from the didactic tradition of declarative instruction and setting up the conditions of genuine apprenticeship.

Suppose a group of parents, teachers, and pastors want to design a school program around particular religious values. It may be difficult for some to give up the belief that children learn these values chiefly by sitting still and listening to someone talk about them. But in fact that's not the best way for children to learn values. If they sit and listen they may learn to recite back their teacher's words, but they won't be learning how to live by certain principles. They need to acquire skills in special kinds of problem solving, decision making, and faith keeping. Program planners will probably also want them to acquire the skills of studying religious history and traditions, so that they will continue to pursue them throughout their lives. The students are essentially apprentices in a religious tradition.

One way of beginning to design a program would be to review the curriculum examples in Chapter 4. There may be a good religious novel for children that could serve as the central focus of a curriculum similar in principle to the Desperate Journey. Through such a book students would come to understand, relive, and solve problems faced by real children early in the history of their religion; they might also learn to recognize contemporary versions of similar issues.

Through such a curriculum the children learn some of the archaeological and historical techniques that real professionals use in studying early religious cultures and in validating relics. Professionals could be invited to visit the school and to bring slides and artifacts. Children could go on digs and visit museums, and science and technology programs could be designed to follow what the children were learning in other parts of the curriculum. It might become a challenge to keep up with the children's interest in photographic, chemical, and microscopic techniques, but together, teachers and students could learn how to use new technologies, how to write reports, and how to put on demonstrations and slide shows of their own.

Basic skills programs—reading, writing, and arithmetic, as sketched in Chapter 6—can be keyed to such projects. When skills are taught within the framework of project goals that provide incentives of their own, children practice more. Spontaneous practice far exceeds what has been assigned when children want to develop skills that really matter to them—skills that they plan to use immediately.

Apprenticeship programs and curriculum packages. Once your program is up and running, a plan for apprenticing prospective teachers and for packaging curriculum guidelines will be needed. The exact ways of doing this will depend upon many factors: the size and nature of the model, the number of training applicants, school district rules, and so on. The general principle, however, is that prospective teachers should be brought in as apprentices. They will need to learn everything sooner or later, so it doesn't matter very much exactly how their training experiences are sequenced. What does matter is that they are given ample time for reflection and discussion. Their supervisors will want to make sure that they are extracting principles from their experiences and learning when and how to apply them. Apprentices should move toward greater independence and assumption of responsibility. Ideally, by the time the training program is finished, the apprentices are able to run the classroom by themselves.

All this takes time, and the exact amount of time will depend upon the degree of previous training the apprentices have had. An experienced, innovative teacher can pick up the principles in a matter of weeks. A novice teacher will probably need a year. Some of the basic skills programs may require additional special training, perhaps even course work at a university. Apprentices need to be provided with both the subskills required to teach various aspects of the program and the integrative skills needed to run the program as a whole.

The first question regarding curriculum packages again will be: how much experience have prospective teachers had? If they are accustomed to dealing with commercial curriculum packages or if they routinely develop lesson units of their own, they will need only some general guidelines. It is usually the case, nevertheless, that a few sample "scripts" are very helpful, even for highly experienced teachers. Dialogues demonstrate exactly how the teachers interact with pupils—answering questions, guiding discussions, providing organization, and steering and coaching. Scripts are especially necessary if the materials are intended for use by novice teachers.

Most working groups have at least one member who is skilled at writing and editing, and perhaps another member who is good at page design and illustration. Materials should be prepared as professionally as possible.

Teacher training and curriculum writing, in addition to spreading a program, force its progenitors to become more fully aware of what they may be doing intuitively. This is another example of the reflection and articulation processes that are central to good apprenticeships and that are required of students, as well.

DECISIONS

With these objectives—forming a like-minded working group of diversified experts, designing an apprenticeship program that incorporates the values and objectives of the group, and preparing a dissemination plan—which of the three routes should be followed? Is it best to work within existing classrooms in ongoing public or private schools? Start a new school? Teach one's children at home?

Working within the system. Ideally, for reasons both philosophical and practical, it is best to work within an existing school system. Philosophically, citizens, whose votes and taxes or private tuition support a school system, should safeguard their investment as well as their democratic ideals. Practically, many of the people who best know how to improve an existing system are already working inside it. The question is whether the rules and regulations of the existing school bureaucracy will permit these talented people to produce new educational models.

Teachers or school administrators will know the answer to this question, or at least know how to find an answer. For those who do not work within the school system, some general guidelines can be mentioned.

An appointment with a local school principal is a good place to begin. Questions to be asked might include: How are textbooks selected? By the school district? By a committee of teachers? By a state board? How much choice do individual teachers and schools have? The answers will vary widely among districts and states. In the most restrictive cases, a textbook must be on a state-approved list, and this list will only periodically be reviewed—perhaps not for three or four years. Every classroom in the state may thus be locked into particular books for a three- or four-year period.

A much more desirable plan is the one adopted by the Christina District in Delaware. A committee of local teachers has reviewed and selected sets of books on literature, spelling, handwriting, and reading—books that they feel are among the best available. Any teacher who wants to use textbooks and needs advice on which ones to choose can consult this list and talk to the teachers who compiled it. Alternatively, any teacher who does not want to use the textbooks and prefers to work directly with children's literature like *The Desperate Journey* is given a budget of somewhere between $30 and $40 per child for the purchase of language arts materials.

A second set of questions concerns curriculum design. Again the answer may be that such decisions are made by state or local committees. The flexibility retained by an individual teacher is important to determine.

It is also important to discover how the curriculum objectives are defined and how levels of competency are measured. Are there tests that students must take? Are they local, statewide, or national tests? Can an individual teacher or an individual school decide what the tests should be?

Sometimes required tests are extensive and detailed, and most of the curriculum will have to be devoted to preparing students for them. But sometimes these tests are minimal, and teachers can easily incorporate, in an otherwise flexible classroom program, the basic information that the tests cover. It may be possible for teachers to arrange alternative ways of evaluating student knowledge—ways that can still convince school boards and legislatures that standards are being maintained.

"Competency demonstration through exhibition" is a phrase introduced by Theodore Sizer and his colleagues in their studies of American high schools.[2] Sizer encourages school reform through various coalitions of school, policy, and teacher-training groups. Frank Murray has been active in efforts in Delaware to adapt Sizer's ideas for elementary schools, and has had this to say about competency exhibitions:

Mastery of the essential intellectual skills, academic information, and knowledge that come to define the school's particular curriculum should be demonstrated by the pupils in as direct and immediate fashion as possible. Pupils should be expected to demonstrate and exhibit what they know by doing it directly, rather than by the indirect demonstrations they are required to make on the usual "paper and pencil" school examination. The important things the pupils have mastered should be apparent in works they can exhibit, in things they can make, compose, design, in the real and personally significant problems they can solve, in the stories they can tell and write, and so forth. The demonstration of recently acquired knowledge through artificial school tasks, tasks that are unlikely to occur very often elsewhere in life, should be replaced by real world tasks that can reveal, often more effectively, what the pupil truly knows and can do.[3]

Some classroom teachers are beginning to implement this method of competency testing.

If the information gained from principals and others locally about textbook selection, curriculum design, and competency testing indicates that teachers have wide opportunities for individualized program development, it may well be feasible to develop new educational models within the public system. Some in the system may already be engaged in such efforts and may, depending on the skills and resources needed, welcome another participant or be willing to participate in a new project.

It may seem, however, that interested teachers, administrators, and parents would have great difficulty in developing a new local program. If this is the case it is important to go still further in gathering information—to higher levels of the hierarchy, the district superintendent's office and the state school board.

Experts at these levels may have different answers to

the same questions already posed locally. District superintendents may know of particular principals or particular teachers who have found ways to implement their own models. There may be special state or federally sponsored alternative schools that are developing new models. One of Sizer's programs, Re: Learning, enables selected schools to bypass district regulations that would otherwise prevent them from developing new classroom models. All possibilities should be explored.

Starting your own school. Starting a school requires teachers, students, parents, a place to work, some supplies, and a genuine willingness to work together and to learn from one another. The philosophy of one such school, the Newark Center for Creative Learning, begun over twenty years ago, was summarized as follows:

> We believe that schools should be staffed by thoughtful, sympathetic teachers who care deeply about each other, the children, and their families. Recognizing that mutual confidence and respect are essential to any good teaching-learning relationship, we hope to be *whole* people to each other. We try to share openly at school the full range of human feelings—amusement, affection, anger, sorrow, appreciation, curiosity, regret.
> . . . We believe that as children mature they need opportunities to learn effective ways to make an impact on the world in which they live so that they can grow to see themselves as useful, purposeful individuals. We hope to help them become aware of the stake that they have in the world and the power that they have to change things.
> We believe that this school is but one in a series of educational situations experienced by our children. They come to us with already well-developed personalities, value priorities, and strategies for learning. If the

school experience is to have full meaning, school families and teachers must share an understanding and appreciation of each others' past experiences and of each others' hopes and aspirations for the future. Learning is not confined to the four walls of a building. School is all that a child's life encompasses. We believe that there can be no manual for teaching living and learning in our school. Each day is in a sense a fresh new adventure bringing achievements and frustrations, success and disappointments. We will all try to learn from each other in order to meet the next day with greater knowledge and wisdom.[4]

I have quoted this statement at length to emphasize the crucial importance of the relationships among the people who decide to get together and start a school. The business and financial side, though obviously important, is secondary. If the interpersonal principles described above can be put into operation, ways can be found to solve the business problems. If these principles cannot be put into operation, then there is little point in addressing the business issues. A new school is people. It is not a system, a manual, a set of bylaws, or a ledger.

Of course a new school can and must function on a sound business footing. It must obey fire regulations and various other local, state, and federal laws, deal with taxes and exemptions, grant opportunities, cost-of-living formulas, utility options, trash removal, libraries, transportation, school lunches, athletics, recruiting, public relations, admissions, and dismissals. But a working group to found a school will include people who are either expert in these matters or willing to make themselves expert in them.[5] What is critical is that the members of the group be willing to learn from each other, and to respect alternative styles of thinking and working.

The group's business experts, for example, are likely to talk about general principles of good management and to express horror at what they term "school inefficiencies." Such an approach may initially alarm some of the humanists in the group. If, however, they investigate those managerial and financial principles, perhaps by consulting local plant managers, they will find very interesting new developments in the industrial world—cooperative methods of managing organizations. Experts in these methods may be able to provide practical guidelines for working together to maintain a school on a sound business footing. One important new management principle involves eliminating layers of expensive middle management. In a school, this means that there need not be an elaborate budget for department heads, deans, curriculum directors, admissions directors, coordinators, and so on. It may be possible to rotate who is doing what. If a school is a true apprenticeship environment, everyone, adults as well as children, will need to learn how to handle a variety of school functions. The point is to listen to one another, to respect one another, to learn from one another, and to seek cooperative solutions. If the group can do that, the experience of starting a new school may well be more rewarding than anyone has even imagined.

Educating children at home. If neither working within an ongoing school system nor starting a school seems feasible, then home schooling may be the best alternative. Home schooling is an interesting and growing phenomenon, though due to the difficulty of collecting statistics, no one is quite sure how widespread it is. A 1987 report estimated that "the actual number of children in home instruction seems to have grown from about 15,000 in the early seventies to well over 120,000 today—perhaps as many as 260,000. (These numbers may seem high, but they represent less than 1% of the total school-age population.) These estimates are based on reports from organizations that supply curricular materials and support, and are supplemented by interviews and questionnaires that provide some measure of the numbers of parents who do not rely on such organizations."[6]

In deciding whether or not to educate children at home, the most important prerequisite is a deep desire to do so. Parents must be ruthlessly (if privately) honest with themselves about how much time they really want to spend with their children. Teaching requires time and hard work, and it must be taken seriously.

But teaching at home has many benefits, as well. Home schooling strengthens family ties and the role of the family in children's lives. One mother comments, "I think that home schooling gives the home more dignity and importance because it is the most important place and the center for everything . . . Our home is a learning center and not just a stopping off station to come home and eat and sleep and get up and work."[7] This also has the effect of making parenting—because most often the mother is the home teacher—more important than it is often felt to be:

> I think that something for me that was really appealing, and I've learned more as I've gotten into it, is that for me, I have a really important role. Not that I feel that I'm missing out on any important roles or anything—you know, being a mother—but not only am I a diaper changer, but I'm a teacher. Not that I have a teaching degree, but even thinking about that role is real special. I get really excited about it—the planning and the teaching.[8]

For career-oriented parents the decision to switch to home teaching as a career (at least for a few years) can hold some unexpected joys:

The way our relationships have improved is real exciting. Back in the old days I was sacrificing everything for my career. So it's been a real about face to change my priorities around and have the family be as important as it is. It's been interesting watching me change, because I would be about the last candidate I would ever have expected to be doing any of this kind of stuff—being a mother and all this high-involvement kind of stuff.[9]

It should not be assumed that a parent's other career interests have to be sacrificed. On the contrary, the involvement of children in parental careers can be an important aspect of home schooling. A working mother describes her experience:

One of the best times we had, in the euphoric first two months out of school, was a marathon session in the biochemistry lab where I work. I had a forty-eight-hour experiment going which had to be checked in the middle of the night. J went in with me the first night and we had trouble with one of the machines, a fraction collector which moves test tubes along under the end of a length of fine tubing which slowly spits out the stuff to be collected. We stayed there until 5 A.M. and J occupied himself almost the whole time with a stopwatch checking the rate of drips from the tubing, the rate of movement of the tubes, and the rate of a monitoring pen on another machine—all work that was necessary for getting the job done—and he revelled in it.

We left the building just as the last stars were leaving the sky. Sheep and cattle were grazing quietly on nearby university pastures. Only the birds provided sound. J was amazed that he had really passed through all the dark hours without sleeping. I thought of all the kids who could not have the kind of exhilaration he had just had because of their confinement to hours dictated to them by schools.

We slept all that morning and went back to the lab for checks during the afternoon and again at night and the following day. J wanted to stay with it right to the end and did. He learned all sorts of things in that short span of time about units of volume and time, about multiplying and dividing, about fractions, about light absorption, magnets, solutions and probably other things. The same boy had been completely turned off by school math and was regarded by some as "slow" and "lazy."[10]

In addition to strengthening family bonds, home schooling enables a type of educational program that is exactly suited to the children involved. It is possible to respond, for example, to a child's desire for knowledge in a way that is difficult or impossible in a classroom of twenty-five children with a mandated curriculum:

I guess it was just the feeling that he would be so stifled if he had to start leaving home at 5 or 4 or 3 like some kids do and have to listen to his teacher instead of finding out all the things he wants to. There's no way we could say, "Well, when you're 6 or when you're 7, you'll just have to be quiet and listen to Dick and Jane and all of that." Knowing him, and knowing how he learned, it was just a natural outgrowth of that . . . He gets something on his mind . . . like he heard about earthquakes in Sunday School. So the whole day, he wanted to know about earthquakes. So finally we had to break out a geology book that I had in college and look at earthquakes. He was asking all sorts of questions, why this and why that, and what is this. He was the same way with volcanoes. He wants to ask questions and he wants to know.[11]

It is also possible to take special account of concerns for an individual child's emotional well-being, as these parents describe:

We felt that he was very immature, and he was in a school where the curriculum was very advanced. We thought that comparing him with other children would not be good, even though he was doing well—average or above—we took that into consideration. We felt that he would fall further and further behind. It was highly competitive, and that isn't his nature, so we didn't feel he could thrive in that.[12]

For those who are willing to make the commitment, and who believe that they can provide a type of educational environment in which their children will thrive, home schooling may be a route to consider very seriously.

The home curriculum. Many people who educate their children at home do so because they hold very strongly to particular philosophical or religious principles. These range from extremely liberal, child-centered, Rousseau-type views, to extremely conservative, doctrine-centered, authoritarian views, with all kinds of variation in between. Organizations that supply home-schooling materials and support, therefore, may favor a particular viewpoint. It is important not to be put off by this. As I have spent this book detailing, some learning environments facilitate the acquisition of knowledge, and others do not. This is true whether one is teaching Darwin's theory of evolution or a biblical view of special creation. The fact is that good guidelines to the techniques of home schooling are independent of the philosophy that their author may want to transmit. Those who are involved in teaching at home should pick out messages they find helpful and pass by expressions of a philosophy they may not share.[13]

Home schooling falls immediately and inevitably into an apprenticeship pattern. Everyone works together on a variety of projects and chores dictated by individual and community interests and economic factors. Planning the home curriculum should be a joint undertaking, with the children fully involved. What could be a major long-term objective? A trip to Yellowstone? Building a boat? Planting a garden? Making a wardrobe of clothes for a doll? Painting a mural? Earning money to buy a computer? Together, teacher and student can block out stages in the project and decide approximately how much time each stage will involve.

Once a framework has been set up, the teacher can turn to the question of the basic skills that will need to be mastered. A good way to begin is to obtain listings of the competencies that the local school district wants the children at each grade level to have achieved. Given that third graders are supposed to master fractions, for example, how are fractions involved in building a boat? In planning a trip to Yellowstone? Daily practice on fractions can be couched in terms of those practical problems. The children need to know what the school district will be expecting of them. Put up a chart somewhere. Some home teachers find that their children whiz by the year-end grade criteria in a matter of months, just for the fun of it.

Those who are new to teaching may be alarmed by the prospect of having to teach something that they don't know very much about. One alternative is to seek out an expert in the subject. Teacher and children can then learn together—perhaps by taking music lessons together, or art lessons, or weaving lessons. Or a teacher may arrange for a college student majoring in geology to come over for a few hours and explain the bubbling mudpots of Yellowstone. It is also possible to join forces with another family or two and share teaching responsibilities.

Legal matters. Every state in the union permits home education in some form, and only a few of them (Iowa, Michigan, and North Dakota, at last count) require home teachers to be certified. States regulate home schooling to different degrees, however, and it is important to find out exactly what the rules are in each case. Some states require children taught at home to be tested periodically, which is a good idea because it relieves the home teacher's worry that her children are falling behind. Some states require registration as a private school, even though just one family may be involved. There appear to be ripples of new legislation favoring home schooling, including repeals of old truancy laws, spreading across the United States. The general import seems to be that though the state has an interest in making sure that all children are educated, its interest doesn't extend to mandating exactly how they are educated. New legislation is supporting the family's freedom to determine the means by which the state's interest is realized.[14]

THE RISKS AND REWARDS OF CHANGE

Teams of individuals *can* improve larger educational environments—by reorganizing existing schools, starting new schools, or developing home educational programs. These routes are not for the faint-hearted or the thin-skinned, of course. As I said at the beginning of this chapter, the schools we have today are the schools most people want. Anyone who speaks in favor of school innovation, however tactfully, will be perceived by many teachers and school administrators to be implying that they have not been doing a good job and by many parents to be implying that they have been derelict in their educational responsibilities toward their own children. With such perceptions in the minds of one's listeners, a fair amount of unfriendly reaction may be anticipated.

Such reactions are one reason I have emphasized the importance of assembling a diversified team, producing a model that people can come and see, and accepting responsibility for training and dissemination. This says to people—to parents, teachers, school administrators, and other concerned citizens—that the model builders' focus is not upon what anyone is doing wrong but upon the design and development of innovations that they hope everyone will enjoy, appreciate, and want to encourage and share.

Conclusion

In 1939, I was one of thousands of excited children who attended the World's Fair just outside New York City and moved, entranced, through General Motor's Futurama exhibit. Recently, a television program looked back at the exhibit's predictions and chronicled their accuracy. A striking aspect of the report was the small amount of prediction that had been devoted to education.[1]

Today, fifty years later, the same caution is apparent. Combing the library for books on social and political forces that affect schools, one finds many commentaries on past and present, but very few that predict how these forces might shape tomorrow's schools.[2] An exception is *Schools of the Future: How American Business and Education Can Cooperate to Save Our Schools* (1985). This book, prepared by Marvin Cetron, president of Forecasting International, and colleagues, was commissioned by the American Association of School Administrators, the major professional organization for American principals and school superintendents.[3]

This last fact is notable. If school administrators accept Cetron's prophecies, they are in a position to foster the implementation of his proposals and thus help effect the changes he anticipates. Hence we should pay close attention to the nature of the business-education partnerships that Cetron foresees, and that are beginning to be widely reported in the news media and other publications.[4]

I am paying especially close attention because I recognize that such partnerships can be viewed as a natural outgrowth of the cognitive apprenticeship principles advocated here. The workplace, after all, gave birth to apprenticeship programs. When the workplace was abandoned as the basic educational environment and replaced by the classroom, we had what Collins and Brown call the "first educational revolution," as mentioned in Chapter 3. The return to workplace instructional models, augmented by principles derived from contemporary cognitive and developmental science, is what the "second educational revolution" is all about.

School-business partnerships could provide a natural arena for the second revolution—for the transformation of traditional, Thorndikean educational environments into meaningful places that prepare youngsters for the kinds of decision making that adult citizens must actually do. Such a transformation, however, is not likely to occur unless program designers apply the principles summarized in this book.

For example, suppose a business organization wants to collaborate with a high school to develop a work-study program. A common approach in such cases is to divide the program into two parts—an academic part that the school handles, and a practical part that the business firm handles. Typically, mastery of the academics is a prerequisite for entry into the job. But there may be very few connections between the academic material that is taught and the practical skills that are needed. It is usually assumed that widely applicable general knowledge is imparted by schools. In fact, as we have seen, school knowledge is usually fractionated into small, disconnected, declarative bits that are specific to particular lessons, teachers, and examinations. Similarly, job routines, especially for beginners, may also be fractionated. Since academic teachers and job supervisors—experts with years of experience—often find it very difficult to work out the connections between the academic bits and the workplace bits, it doesn't make much sense to expect inexperienced students to be able to do so. It is much more likely that the academic training in such a work-study program will be almost totally useless from a practical point of view, except that it may instill habits of conformity to daily routines. Worse, since the academic training will have to be crammed into a shorter time frame in order to leave room for workplace training, students in joint programs will risk learning even less in school than they are learning today.

Suppose, however, that an energetic, creative team from the school and the workplace (with perhaps even a few talented outsiders and consultants) got together and designed an integrated work-study program. Suppose that this team spent a number of months wrestling with the question of just what kind of apprenticeship program would best develop skilled, adaptable citizens—students who understood that the job competency they were acquiring was intimately connected to the economy and the culture in which they would soon be living as adults. Suppose that the team had a free hand to group and schedule students in the most productive ways, rather than in the ways that best suited the convenience of previous managements—and that what was most productive also proved, not surprisingly, to be cost effective. Suppose that experts from the workplace and experts from the school worked side by side with small groups of youngsters, modeling problem-solving attitudes and inventiveness, demonstrating skills, and cheering them on. What might such a work-study program, and such a school, be like?

As another example, suppose that the managers of an industrial park decided to establish a school for the children of their workers. A typical approach would be to contract with the public school system to put a traditional elementary school on the park grounds. Day-care facilities and afterschool programs for older children would be part of the arrangement. But while this might be more convenient for working parents, such a program would not begin to exploit the profound educational potential of the situation. An energetic, creative design team might instead adopt the guiding principle that early education is primarily a family enterprise and develop programs that would enable parents and children to share learning opportunities. What might these schools be like?

To provide general guidelines for these and other new educational settings that can address and respond to the educational needs I have described in preceding chapters, I review key principles below.

GETTING STARTED

Starting an apprenticeship program involves three major steps. First, a diversified team of experts must be assembled. This should be a working team, which means it should be small and dedicated to getting things done. Designing a school is not unlike putting on a multimedia production. The people who do it must be both talented and efficient. Additionally, they must be able to work together, and enjoy learning from others. They should eschew bureaucratic buildup in their own ranks and in the programs they design.

Second, the team must work out detailed plans for a genuine apprenticeship program. This involves dealing with difficult questions about what kinds of skills students are really expected to develop, and what kinds of experiences and practice opportunities must therefore be provided. It is important to think these matters through in depth.

Third, once the program is running successfully, the team must work out mechanisms for disseminating it. This will typically involve apprenticeship-type training programs for teachers and other personnel, and also the production of written guidelines and other materials. The dissemination responsibilities will assist the team to clarify, evaluate, and revise its program.

THE PARTS RELATED TO THE WHOLE

An apprenticeship program must maintain its holistic approach in all of its component activities. Every activity should be explicitly related to and derived from a project that is moving toward a goal. This means, too, that each activity should be clearly connected to other activities. Students should always understand how an immediate activity relates to an overall project and its development.

Students should be grouped on the basis of their interests and skills rather than on the basis of administrative convenience. Students who know that they are making important contributions to meaningful projects will rarely be discipline problems.

Students should participate in determining their own

evaluation procedures. Summative evaluations should probe the full roster of students' knowledge, not merely their declarative knowledge.

BASIC SKILLS AND LARGER PROJECTS

Basic literacy and numeracy programs should operate in the context of larger-scale projects. (This follows, of course, from the principle that activities of any sort should be explicitly connected to important objectives as well as to each other.) Students should acquire not only first-order skills (word recognition, number facts) but also second-order skills of analytical reasoning and logic. Since higher-order skills guide the usage of lower-order skills, they should be taught simultaneously with, or even in advance of, the lower-order skills.

Literacy skills (reading, spelling, etc.) are structurally interconnected, as are numeracy skills (adding, subtracting, etc.). The interconnections should be made explicit to students, so that they are encouraged to see the structure of knowledge—of what they are learning—as a whole.

Students should practice applying basic skills extensively. Such practice should be designed in a way that allows students to discover how to tailor basic skills to new contexts and new problems, and to be inventive.

PROGRAMS

Possibilities for apprenticeship programs are myriad. They may focus on, or interrelate, the domains of the humanities, the social sciences, science, or technology. But whether they involve the exploration of the environment, computers, principles of laboratory science, the history or anthropology of an area, or the arts, such programs all share certain general characteristics. They situate learning in complex, meaningful contexts; they derive instructional objectives from the study of what expert practitioners actually do, and bring expert models into the learning environment; they begin where students begin, with the skills and knowledge that students bring to the learning situation; and they capitalize on the principle that learning is a social enterprise, and that knowledge is distributed across groups.

Apprenticeship instructional techniques emphasize modeling, coaching, scaffolding, and fading. They also require students to reflect upon and articulate their learning experiences, and to explore new domains of skill application.

THEORETICAL GROUNDING

In designing new educational programs, we must make sure that they are grounded in contemporary principles of cognitive and developmental science, and that pedagogical provisions have been made for mechanisms of attention and perception, for working memory and its role in knowledge acquisition, for the different types of long-term knowledge, and for the innate learning capacities of human beings.

In particular, it is crucial to arrange learning environments for the acquisition of procedural, conceptual, analogical, and logical knowledge, rather than concentrating almost exclusively on the acquisition of declarative knowledge.

FROM THE PAST TO THE FUTURE

To design effective educational environments, we must study the traditions and forces that have led to present-day school practice, including the child-centered tradition, behavioral science of the early twentieth century, and the early (mis)applications of assembly-line industrial principles to schools. We must become aware of the fetters of outmoded tradition, but we must not lose sight of productive continuities.

As I write these words, it is the first week in September. I am in a small college town. Banners are up, welcoming students. Stores are freshly stocked with book bags, calendars, pencil cases, soon-to-be-sharpened pencils, and composition books. Near the campus, a high school band is holding its first practice. Through the windows of the elementary school, teachers can be seen busily arranging their rooms. School buses are being polished. A shared current of anticipation runs through everyone as the first day of school approaches. The town hums with it. The nation hums with it.

Within a month, that excitement will be over. In some hearts it will never reawaken. The tedium will have set in. All too many students will have been told to disconnect—to turn off their minds and their experiences, and to replace them with an endless series of arbitrary exercises that will be counted, graded, and stacked. They will be serving as passive apprentices in an insular bureaucratic system, learning to play, more or less successfully, a role essential to the maintenance of the system—the role of "the pupil." They will almost never have the opportunity to serve as apprentices in the types of real-world problem-solving, decision-making systems that they will enter as adults.

We know how to fix this. The expertise exists: we know how to design learning environments that nurture mental development and that ultimately produce good thinkers who can reason productively about the cultural, scientific, and technological forces that converge on the lives of citizens of the world and their families. The question is whether we will make the decision to use that expertise now.

Notes
Suggested Reading
Credits
Index

Notes

INTRODUCTION

1. *A Nation at Risk* (Washington, D.C.: U.S. Government Printing Office, 1983), p. 1.
2. *Reading Report Card: Trends in Reading of Four National Assessments, 1971–1984*, National Assessment of Educational Progress, report no. 15–R–01 (Princeton, N.J.: Educational Testing Service, 1986), table 2.1, p. 16.
3. Edward B. Fiske, "American Students Score Average or Below in International Math Exams," *New York Times,* September 23, 1984.
4. *National Report on College Bound Seniors,* published yearly by the Educational Testing Service, Princeton, N.J.
5. Larry Rohter, "The Scourge of Adult Illiteracy," *New York Times: Education Life,* April 13, 1986, p. 35.
6. James B. Hunt, "Action for Excellence: Excerpts from the Task Force on Education for Economic Growth," *Educational Leadership,* September 1983, p. 16. For a more recent discussion, see Stuart Rosenfeld's "Educating for the Factories of the Future," in *Education Week,* June 22, 1988, p. 48.
7. John Goodlad, *A Place Called School: Prospects for the Future* (New York: McGraw-Hill, 1984), p. 468.
8. Harry L. Gracey, *Curriculum or Craftsmanship: Elementary School Teachers in a Bureaucratic System* (Chicago: University of Chicago Press, 1972), pp. 177–179, 183.
9. Quoted in Edward B. Fiske, "Beyond the Classroom,"

Education: Spring Survey, New York Times, April 14, 1985, p. 43. Shanker developed these ideas further, and proposed a reform mechanism, in an article by Lynn Olson entitled "Saying Reforms Fail Most Pupils, Shanker Argues for a 'New Type' of Teaching Unit," *Education Week,* April 6, 1988, p. 1.

10. Eugene Linden, "An Old Idea Makes a Comeback: Apprenticeship Helps Teach the Skill of Problem Solving," *Time,* June 12, 1989.

1 / WHERE OUR SCHOOLS ARE COMING FROM

1. H. L. Gracey, *Curriculum or Craftsmanship* (Chicago: University of Chicago Press, 1972), provides an insightful overview of the two approaches to education highlighted in this chapter.
2. Jean-Jacques Rousseau, *Emile, or Education* (1762; New York: Dutton, 1911), p. 141.
3. S. Alexander Rippa, *Education in a Free Society* (New York: David McKay, 1967), p. 53.
4. Rousseau, *Emile,* p. 134.
5. Philippe Ariès, *Centuries of Childhood: A Social History of Family Life,* trans. Robert Baldick (New York: Random House, 1962).
6. Lawrence A. Cremin, *The Transformation of the School* (New York: Random House, 1964).
7. P. A. Schilpp, ed., *The Philosophy of John Dewey* (Evanston: Northwestern University Press, 1939); A. G. Wirth, *John Dewey as Educator* (New York: John Wiley, 1966).
8. H. J. Perkinson, *Two Hundred Years of American Educational Thought* (New York: David McKay, 1976).
9. Katherine Camp Mayhew and Anna Camp Edwards, *The Dewey School* (New York: Appleton-Century, 1936).
10. Ibid., p. 61. The original was set in italic.
11. Ibid., pp. 68–69.
12. Ibid., pp. 77–78.
13. Ibid., pp 120–122.
14. Ibid., pp. 222–223.

15. John Dewey, *The Child and the Curriculum* (Chicago: University of Chicago Press, 1902), p. 42.
16. Raymond E. Callahan, *Education and the Cult of Efficiency* (Chicago: University of Chicago Press, 1962), p. 129.
17. The paradoxical factors involved in the belief that child development could be fostered through factorylike regimentation (which is still characteristic of our educational system, as I will discuss in Chapter 7) have been examined in Ronald Cohen and Raymond Mohl, *The Paradox of Progressive Education* (Port Washington, N.Y.: National University Publications, 1979).
18. Geraldine Joncich, *The Sane Positivist: A Biography of Edward L. Thorndike* (Middletown: Wesleyan University Press, 1968).
19. The official version of this often-paraphrased statement is in an essay by Thorndike that appeared in the *Seventeenth Yearbook of the National Society for the Study of Education* (Bloomington, 1918), p. 16.
20. Edward L. Thorndike, *The Psychology of Arithmetic* (New York: Macmillan, 1922), p. 13.

2 / THE ADVENT OF COGNITIVE SCIENCE

1. See Howard Gardner, *The Mind's New Science* (New York: Basic Books, 1985).
2. Audrey Champagne and Joan Rogalska-Saz, "Computer-Based Numeration Instruction," technical report, Learning Research and Development Center, University of Pittsburgh, 1988.
3. For an overview of early contributions of artificial intelligence, see Avron Barr, Paul Cohen, and Edward Feigenbaum, eds., *The Handbook of Artificial Intelligence*, 3 vols. (Los Altos, Calif.: Kaufmann, 1981). Recent developments in areas known variously as "neural networks," "parallel distributed processing systems," "computational models," and "connectionism" are summarized in David Rumelhart and James McClelland, eds., *Parallel Distributed Processing: Exploration in the Mi-*

crostructure of Cognition, 2 vols. (Cambridge, Mass.: MIT Press, 1986).

4. Seminal research on computer models of dyslexia has been conducted by Geoffrey E. Hinton and Time Shallice, "Lesioning a Connectionist Network: Investigations of Acquired Dyslexia," technical report CRG–TR–89–3, Department of Computer Science, University of Toronto, 10 Kings College Road, Toronto M5S 1A4, Canada; K. E. Patterson, M. S. Seidenberg, and J. L. McClelland, "Connections and Disconnections: Acquired Dyslexia in a Computational Model of Reading," in *Parallel Distributed Processing: Implications for Psychology and Neurobiology,* ed. R. G. M. Morris (Oxford: Oxford University Press, in press); and M. S. Seidenberg and J. L. McClelland, "A Distributed, Developmental Model of Word Recognition and Naming," *Psychological Review,* in press.

5. The following summary draws from many sources but is essentially my own synthesis. The literature in question is extremely large. For original sources, see Donald Norman, ed., *Perspectives on Cognitive Science* (Norwood, N.J.: Ablex, 1981), a collection of papers presented at the first meeting of the Cognitive Science Society. For more detailed background, consult William Estes, ed., *Handbook of Learning and Cognitive Processes,* vol. 4, *Attention and Memory,* vol. 5, *Human Information Processing,* and vol. 6, *Linguistic Functions in Cognitive Theory* (Hillsdale, N.J.: Erlbaum, 1978). Seminal work on human memory and many other facets of the cognitive science approach are summarized in Peter Lindsay and Donald Norman, *Human Information Processing* (New York: Academic Press, 1977).

6. Quoted in Frances Yates, *The Art of Memory* (New York: Penguin, 1978), p. 48.

7. My typology of knowledge is derived from the experimental psychology of learning, a field much older than cognitive science. Since the late 1890s, there have been thousands of papers on skill learning, or *procedural learning.* There has also been an extensive exploration of ver-

bal learning, which, with some inclusions from the fields of linguistics and semantics, comprises *declarative learning*. There is an equally extensive tradition of concept learning, sometimes called concept attainment, which utilizes inductive paradigms: *conceptual learning*. What I call *analogical learning* is exemplified by the one-trial recognition paradigms described later in this chapter. *Logic acquisition* has been studied in the experimental literature on problem solving and reasoning, and now includes what some cognitive scientists refer to as "qualitative models," which people construct to explain how something (such as electricity) works. These five different ways of learning produce the five types of knowledge discussed here. It can be argued, of course, that all five types of knowledge are fundamentally the same—that all of them can be thought of as different types of procedural knowledge, for example. It is nevertheless convenient to distinguish them, especially because they have been so clearly distinguished as experimental paradigms and because the distinctions have important implications for instruction. Except for declarative knowledge, all forms of knowledge—procedural, conceptual, analogical, and logical—must be forged from experience. Unless the instructional program provides for experiences, only declarative knowledge will be imparted.

8. S. E. Antell and D. P. Keating, "Perception of Numerical Invariance in Neonates," *Child Development* 54 (1983):695–701; P. Starkey and R. G. Cooper, "Perception of Numbers by Human Infants," *Science* 210 (1980):1033–35.

9. N. Cowan, K. Suomi, and P. A. Morse, "Echoic Storage in Infant Perception," *Child Development* 53 (1982):984–990; R. E. Lasky and D. Spiro, "The Processing of Tachistoscopically Presented Visual Stimuli by Five-Month-Old Infants," *Child Development* 51 (1980):1291–94.

10. M. T. H. Chi, "Age Differences in Memory Span," *Journal of Experimental Child Psychology* 23 (1977):266–281.

11. Robbie Case, "Intellectual Development from Birth to Adulthood: A Neo-Piagetian Interpretation," in *Children's*

Thinking: What Develops? ed. R. S. Siegler (Hillsdale, N.J.: Erlbaum, 1978).

12. M. T. H. Chi, "Speed of Processing: A Developmental Source of Limitation," *Topics in Learning and Learning Disabilities* 2 (1982):23–32; M. E. Ford and D. P. Keating, "Developmental and Individual Differences in Long-Term Memory Retrieval: Process and Organization," *Child Development* 52 (1981):234–241; Robert Kail, "Developmental Functions for Speeds of Cognitive Processes," *Journal of Experimental Child Psychology* 45 (1988):339–364; F. J. Morrison, "The Development of Alertness," *Journal of Experimental Child Psychology* 34 (1982):187–199.

13. George A. Miller and P. M Gildea, "How Children Learn Words," *Scientific American* 257 (1987):94–99.

14. Jerome Bruner, *Toward a Theory of Instruction* (Cambridge, Mass.: Harvard University Press, 1966), pp. 10–11, 18.

15. D. Starkey, "The Origins of Concept Formation: Object Sorting and Object Preference in Early Infancy," *Child Development* 52 (1981):489–497.

16. M. T. H. Chi and R. D. Koeske, "Network Representation of a Child's Dinosaur Knowledge," *Developmental Psychology* 19 (1983):29–39.

17. A. L. Brown and M. S. Scott, "Recognition Memory for Pictures in Preschool Children," *Journal of Experimental Child Psychology* 11 (1971):401–412.

18. Daniel J. Slobin, "Cognitive Prerequisites for the Development of Grammar," in *Studies of Child Language Development*, ed. C. A. Ferguson and D. J. Slobin (New York: Holt, Rinehart and Winston, 1973).

19. Jean Piaget, *The Moral Judgment of the Child* (New York: Macmillan, 1965).

20. M. Hass, "Cognition-in-Context: The Social Nature of the Transformation of Mathematical Knowledge in a Third Grade Classroom," technical report, Social Relations Graduate Program, University of California, Irvine, ca. 1986.

21. Jean Lave, "The Culture of Acquisition and the Practice of Understanding," report no. IRL88–0007, Institute for Re-

search on Learning, 3333 Coyote Hill Road, Palo Alto, Calif. 94304. The quotation is on pp. 12–13.

3 / WHAT OUR SCHOOLS SHOULD BECOME

1. Allan Collins and John Seely Brown, "Cognitive Apprenticeship: The Second Educational Revolution" (in preparation). See also Allan Collins, John Seely Brown, and Susan E. Newman, "Cognitive Apprenticeship: Teaching the Craft of Reading, Writing, and Mathematics," in *Knowing, Learning, and Instruction: Essays in Honor of Robert Glaser*, ed. Lauren B. Resnick (Hillsdale, N.J.: Erlbaum, 1989); John Seely Brown, Allan Collins, and Paul Duguid, "Situated Cognition and the Culture of Learning," *Educational Researcher* 18 (February 1989); Allan Collins, "Cognitive Apprenticeship and Instructional Technology," in *Dimensions of Thinking and Cognitive Instruction*, ed. B. F. Jones and L. Idol (Hillsdale, N.J.: Erlbaum, forthcoming). The work of anthropologist Jean Lave has been especially noted by Collins and Brown in the development of their approach. Some of her publications include: "The Culture of Acquisition and the Practice of Understanding," report no. IRL88–007, Institute for Research on Learning; *Cognition in Practice: Mind, Mathematics, and Culture in Everyday Life* (New York: Cambridge University Press, 1988); and "Tailored Learning: Apprenticeship and Everyday Practice among Craftsmen in West Africa" (in preparation). Other important works Collins and Brown have drawn upon include: Carl Bereiter and Marlene Scardamalia, *The Psychology of Written Composition* (Hillsdale, N.J.: Erlbaum, 1987); Ann L. Brown and Annemarie Palinscar, "Reciprocal Teaching of Comprehension Strategies: A Natural History of One Program for Enhancing Learning," in *Intelligence and Cognition in Special Children: Comparative Studies of Giftedness, Mental Retardation, and Learning Disabilities*, ed. J. B. Borkowski and J. D. Day (Norwood, N.J.: Ablex, 1988); Barbara Rogoff and Jean Lave, eds., *Everyday Cognition: Its Development in a Social*

Context (Cambridge, Mass.: Harvard University Press, 1984); Mark R. Lepper and David Greene, *The Hidden Costs of Reward* (Hillsdale, N.J.: Erlbaum, 1979); Seymour Papert, *Mindstorms: Children, Computers, and Powerful Ideas* (New York: Basic Books, 1980); and Alan H. Schoenfeld, *Mathematical Problem Solving* (New York: Academic Press, 1985); Alan H. Schoenfeld, "On Mathematics as Sense-Making: An Informal Attack on the Unfortunate Divorce of Formal and Informal Mathematics," in *Informal Reasoning and Education*, ed. David Perkins, J. Segal, and James Voss (Hillsdale, N.J.: Erlbaum, forthcoming).

The work of Collins and Brown and others is also stimulating renewed interest in historical accounts of apprenticeships. An excellent entry into this massive literature is W. J. Rorabaugh, *The Craft Apprentice: From Franklin to the Machine Age in America* (New York: Oxford University Press, 1986).

2. Loren Eiseley, "The Time of Man," in *Darwin and the Mysterious Mr. X* (New York: Dutton, 1979); Harold Fishbein, *Evolution, Development, and Children's Learning* (Pacific Palisades, Calif.: Goodyear Publishing, 1976); H. Jerison, *Evolution of the Brain and Intelligence* (New York: Academic Press, 1973); Alison Jolly, *The Evolution of Primate Behavior* (New York: Macmillan, 1972); Philip Lieberman, *The Biology and Evolution of Language* (Cambridge, Mass.: Harvard University Press, 1984).

3. Carl Bereiter and M. Bird, "Use of Thinking Aloud in Identification and Teaching of Reading Comprehension Strategies," *Cognition and Instruction* (1985):131–156.

4. Merlyn J. Behr, Richard Lesh, Thomas R. Post, and Edward A. Silver, "Rational-Number Concepts," in *Acquisition of Mathematics Concepts and Processes*, ed. Richard Lesh and Marsha Landau (New York: Academic Press, 1983).

5. Roy Pea, "Distributed Intelligence in Learning and Reasoning Processes," paper presented at the annual meeting of the Cognitive Science Society, Montreal, Canada, August 1988.

6. Napoleon A. Chagnon and William Irons, eds., *Evolutionary Biology and Human Social Behavior: An Anthropological Perspective* (Belmont, Calif.: Wadsworth, 1979); Robert A. Hinde, *Biological Bases of Human Social Behavior* (New York: McGraw-Hill, 1974); Lionel Tiger, *Men in Groups* (New York: Random House, 1970).
7. James W. Botkin, Mahdi Elmandjra, and Bircea Malitza, *No Limits to Learning: Bridging the Human Gap* (New York: Pergamon Press, 1979).
8. Ibid., p. 1.
9. Ibid., pp. 12–13.
10. Ibid., pp. 13–14.
11. Daniel Levine and Robert Havighurst, *Society and Education* (Boston: Allyn and Bacon, 1989); Nicholas Appleton, *Cultural Pluralism in Education: Theoretical Foundations* (New York: Longman, 1983).
12. Robert W. Rhodes, "Holistic Teaching/Learning for Native American Students," *Journal of American Indian Education* (January 1988): 21–28.
13. Manuel Ramirez III and Alfredo Castaneda, *Cultural Democracy, Bicognitive Development, and Education* (New York: Academic Press, 1974), p. 142.
14. Ibid., p. 143.
15. Ibid.
16. James Banks, *Multiethnic Education: Theory and Practice* (Boston: Allyn and Bacon, 1988), p. 205.
17. Joe Nathan, *Free to Teach: Achieving Equity and Excellence in Schools* (New York: Pilgrim Press, 1983).

4 / TRANSMITTING THE CULTURE

1. Peter Sutton, ed., *Dreamings: The Art of Aboriginal Australia* (New York: Asia Society Galleries and George Braziller Publishers, 1988).
2. Larry Cuban, *How Teachers Taught: Constancy and Change in American Classrooms, 1890–1980* (New York: Longman, 1984). See also Eliot Wigginton, *Sometimes a Shining Moment: The Foxfire Experience* (New York: Doubleday, 1985).

Wigginton writes, "I have now become convinced that the greatest disservice to education ever to smite the public schools was the wholesale stampede to textbooks as the primary vehicle for learning. It's not that the texts themselves are bad (though many of them are), but the way we use them. They have spread like a cancer inside our classrooms. They have been allowed to dominate everything we do. We have willingly allowed them to rob us of the greatest educational tool of all—the active grappling with the subject matter itself for ends other than its own acquisition; the collective probing of the unknown . . . And there, of course, is the crux of the problem: the relationship between printed information—the accumulated experience of decades—and the accumulated experiences of the students themselves. Quite simply, in too many instances, students just don't know what we or our texts are talking about, or they cannot make any connection between that information and their world. Thus they cannot internalize the information or make use of it, and thus it is discarded as irrelevant as soon as the tests are taken" (p. 207). Wigginton was referring to high school students. On younger children, see David Elkind, *Miseducation* (New York: Knopf, 1987), which addresses the question of whether earlier preparation for textbook learning would help. His answer is negative.

3. Lonna Bush Jones, "Another Way to Learn," *American Education* (May 1981), provides a glimpse of the veritable warehouse of materials developed by a truly remarkable group. The support of Trinity University in San Antonio was crucial for LAL.

4. Julia Jarrell, Susan Monday, and Susan Russell, eds., *Lessons in Looking: Dialogues with O'Neil Ford, Architect* (San Antonio: Learning about Learning Educational Foundation, 1981).

5. Kathleen Fidler, *The Desperate Journey* (North Pomfret, Vt.: David and Charles, 1989); Fred Rendell and Patricia Watterson, *The Desperate Journey: Computer-Assisted Topics* (Glasgow: Jordanhill College of Education, 1985), is the

curriculum manual developed around Fidler's novel. This and many other outstanding materials are listed in the Jordanhill catalog, which can be obtained from Robin Frame, Director, Sales and Publications, Jordanhill College of Education, 76 Southbrae Drive, Glasgow G13 1PP, Scotland.

6. Jordanhill College of Education provides teachers with materials and training courses in the many subskills that enter into large-scale projects like the Desperate Journey. Bill Michael and his colleagues have prepared ten booklets on techniques for guiding children to express ideas through art. Number four is "Time-Lapse Friezes." All may be ordered from the Jordanhill catalog (see note 5).

7. Rendell and Watterson, *The Desperate Journey: Computer-Assisted Topics*, p. 23.

8. Peter Hancock and Robert Long, *Kings and Things* (London: BBC Radio for Schools, 1979).

9. Ibid., p. 12.

10. Kathleen Forsythe and Candace Wedder, "Communication-Based Education: Open Learning for the Classroom," *Proceedings of the Fifth International Conference on Technology and Education*, vol. 1, ed. J. H. Collins, N. Estes, and D. Walker (Edinburgh: CEP Consultants Ltd., 1988); J. W. Johnson, "Education and the New Technology: A Force of History," *Educational Technology* (October 1981); E. C. Posner, "Information and Communication in the Third Millennium," *IEEE Communications Magazine* (January 1979).

11. Randall White, *Dark Caves, Bright Visions: Life in Ice Age Europe* (New York: American Museum of National History, in association with W. W. Norton and Company, 1986).

12. *Man: A Course of Study* was developed by the Education Development Center, Inc., under grants from the National Science Foundation. It is now available through Curriculum Development Associates, Inc., Suite 414, 1211 Connecticut Avenue, Washington, D.C. 20036.

13. In the first sixty pages of *Schools of To-Morrow* (New York:

Dutton, 1915), John Dewey and his coauthor, Evelyn Dewey, quote, amplify, and extoll Rousseau. On page 61, however, they write: "Rousseau, while he was writing his *Emile*, was allowing his own children to grow up entirely neglected by their parents, abandoned in a foundling asylum. It is not strange then that his readers and students should center their interest in his theories, in his general contribution to education, rather than in his account of the impractical methods he used to create that exemplary prig—Emile."

5 / SCIENCE AND TECHNOLOGY

1. Henry Ford with Samuel Crowther, *My Life and Work* (New York: Garden City, 1922), p. 22.
2. Jerome Bruner, "The Nature and Uses of Immaturity," *American Psychologist* 27 (August 1972): 687–708.
3. Jeff Goldberg, *Anatomy of a Scientific Discovery* (New York: Bantam Books, 1988); James D. Watson, *The Double Helix: A Personal Account of the Discovery of the Structure of DNA* (New York: Atheneum, 1968).
4. Deborah C. Smith, "Cognitive Processes and Students' Misconceptions in Science," paper presented to the annual meeting of the Northeastern Educational Research Association, October 25, 1984; Deborah C. Smith and David Johns, "Teaching for Conceptual Change: Rationale and Description of Activities in a First Grade Science Unit," paper presented to the annual meeting of the Northeastern Education Research Association, October 24, 1985.
5. G. Posner, K. Strike, P. Hewson, and W. Gertzog, "Accommodation of a Scientific Conception: Toward A Theory of Conceptual Change," *Science Education* 66 (1982):211–227; E. L. Smith, "Teaching for Conceptual Change: Some Ways of Going Wrong," pp. 57–66 in *Proceedings of the International Seminar on Misconceptions in Science and Mathematics*, ed. H. Helm and J. Novak (Ithaca: Cornell University Press, 1983).

6. George E. Forman and David S. Kuschner, *The Child's Construction of Knowledge: Piaget for Teaching Children* (Monterey, Calif.: Wadsworth, 1977); Constance Kamii and Rheta DeVries, *Physical Knowledge in Preschool Education: Implications of Piaget's Theory* (Englewood Cliffs, N.J.: Prentice-Hall, 1978).
7. Jean Piaget, "The Problem of Shadows," in *The Child's Conception of Physical Causality* (London: Routledge and Kegan Paul, 1951).
8. Barbara Y. White and Paul Horwitz, "ThinkerTools: Enabling Children to Understand Physical Laws," report no. 6470, BBN Laboratories, Bolt, Beranek and Newman, Inc., 10 Moulton Street, Cambridge, Mass. 02138.
9. Allan Collins and John Seely Brown, "The Computer as a Tool for Learning through Reflection," in *Learning Issues for Intelligent Tutoring Systems,* ed. H. Mandl and A. Lesgold (New York: Springer, forthcoming); Allan Collins, "Cognitive Apprenticeship and Instructional Technology" in *Dimensions of Thinking and Cognitive Instruction,* ed. B. F. Jones and L. Idol (Hillsdale, N.J.: Erlbaum, forthcoming).

6 / BASIC SKILLS

1. I. J. Gelb, *A Study of Writing* (Chicago: University of Chicago Press, 1963).
2. R. M. Shiffrin, "Capacity Limitations in Information Processing, Attention, and Memory," in *Handbook of Learning and Cognitive Processes,* vol. 4, ed. W. K. Estes (Hillsdale, N.J.: Erlbaum, 1976); R. M Shiffrin and S. T. Dumais, "The Development of Automatism," in *Cognitive Skills and Their Acquisition,* ed. J. R. Anderson (Hillsdale, N.J.: Erlbaum, 1981).
3. J. J. Murphy, *The Rhetorical Tradition and Modern Writing* (New York: Language Association of America, 1982).
4. C. W. Griffin, "Programs for Writing across the Curriculum: A Report," *College Composition and Communication* 36 (1985): 398–403; R. Parker, "Language across the Curric-

ulum Movement: A Brief Overview and Bibliography," *College Composition and Communication* (1985): 173–177.

5. Sylvia Ashton-Warner, *Teacher* (New York: Bantam, 1963); Donald H. Graves, *Writing: Teachers and Children at Work* (London: Heinemann, 1983); Donald M. Murray, *Read to Write: A Writing Process Reader* (New York: Holt, Rinehart and Winston, 1986).

6. T. L. Harris and E. J. Cooper, eds., *Reading, Thinking, and Concept Development* (New York: College Board, 1985), is an excellent collection of research summaries with guidelines for practicing listening and reading comprehension skills.

7. Carl Bereiter and Marlene Bird, "Use of Thinking Aloud in Identification and Teaching of Reading Comprehension Strategies," *Cognition and Instruction* 2 (1985): 131–156.

8. Fred Rendell and Patricia Watterson, *The Desperate Journey: Computer-Assisted Topics* (Glasgow: Jordanhill College of Education, 1985), p. 48.

9. Donald Graves, *Writing: Teachers and Children at Work* (London: Heinemann, 1983).

10. Linda Flower, John R. Hayes, L. Carey, K. Schriver, and J. Stratman, "Detection, Diagnosis and the Strategies of Revision," *College Composition and Communication* 37 (1986): 16–55; Donald M. Murray, "Internal Revision: A Process of Discovery," in *Research on Composing: Points of Departure*, ed. C. R. Cooper and L. Odell (Urbana: National Council of Teachers of English, 1978); M. I. Sommers, "Revision Strategies of Student Writers and Experienced Writers," *College Composition and Communication* 31 (1980): 378–387.

11. Carl Bereiter and Marlene Scardamalia, *The Psychology of Written Composition* (Hillsdale, N.J.: Erlbaum, 1987), esp. chap. 11.

12. Gelb, *A Study of Writing*, p. 185.

13. On the orthographic cipher, see C. Juel, P. L. Griffith, and P. B. Gough, "Acquisition of Literacy: A Longitudinal Study of Children in First and Second Grade," *Journal*

of Educational Psychology 78 (1986): 243–255. Robert C. Aukerman, *Approaches to Beginning Reading* (New York: John Wiley, 1984), is a feisty review of hundreds of reading methods. See especially Aukerman's reflections on phonics, pp. 244–246. Some readers may be embroiled in controversies over teaching phonics. Commercial phonics programs are typically confusing, wrong about the spelling-sound correspondence rules of English, and/or don't provide sufficient practice. It is very common, for example, for a reading lesson to teach a letter-sound rule that never appears in the reading assignment—the story that accompanies the lesson—and the rule may be wrong in any case. It is inappropriate, however, to make a blanket statement about the value of teaching phonics. If children are not learning to read well, parents, teachers, and citizens in general need to be concerned about the entire reading program, including, but not limited to, its phonics component. I have tried to describe in this chapter what I believe a good language arts program should contain.

14. Romalda Spalding and Walter Spalding, *The Writing Road to Reading* (New York: Morrow, 1986). It is important to note that Mrs. Spalding, who is still, at the age of ninety, actively teaching her method, does not concur with some of my interpretations and elaborations. Hence, though we incorporate parts of her system in the program offered by the Reading Study Center at the University of Delaware, we call it by another name—the Intensive Literacy program.

15. The term *phonogram* appears in a reading series called *The Rational Method in Reading*, by Edward Ward, first published in 1894. In more modern terms, these orthographic units have been called *relational units* by linguist Richard Venezky in *The Structure of English Orthography* (The Hague: Mouton, 1970).

16. Extensive research on the role of spelling in teaching reading has been conducted by Linnea Ehri, of the University of California, Davis. See, for example, Linnea Ehri and

Lee Wilce, "Does Learning to Spell Help Beginners Learn to Read Words?" *Reading Research Quarterly* 22 (Winter 1987). The answer to her title question is yes.

17. Alan Schoenfeld, *Mathematical Problem Solving* (New York: Academic Press, 1985).

18. Zoltan Dienes, *Building Up Mathematics* (London: Hutchinson, 1960); Zoltan Dienes, *An Experimental Study of Mathematics-Learning* (London: Hutchinson, 1963); Zoltan Dienes, *The Power of Mathematics* (London: Hutchinson, 1964); Zoltan Dienes, *Mathematics in the Primary School* (New York: Macmillan, 1966). The games described appear in Michael Holt and Zoltan Dienes, *Let's Play Math* (New York: Walker, 1973).

19. Magdalene Lampert, "Knowing, Doing, and Teaching Multiplication," *Cognition and Instruction* 3 (1986):305–342; Herbert P. Ginsburg and Takashi Yamamoto, "Understanding, Motivation, and Teaching: Comments on Lampert's 'Knowing, Doing, and Teaching Multiplication,' " *Cognition and Instruction* (1986):357–370; Herbert P. Ginsburg, *Children's Arithmetic* (Austin, Tex.: PRO-ED, Inc., 1989); Lauren B. Resnick and Wendy W. Ford, *The Psychology of Mathematics for Instruction* (Hillsdale, N.J.: Erlbaum, 1981). On Japanese teaching of mathematics, see Giyoo Hatano, "Learning to Add and Subtract: A Japanese Perspective," in *Addition and Subtraction: A Cognitive Perspective,* ed. Thomas P. Carpenter, James M. Moser, and Thomas A. Romberg (Hillsdale, N.J.: Erlbaum, 1982).

20. For information about Unifix, write to Philograph Publications Ltd., North Way, Andover, Hants, England. See also Catherine Stern, Margaret B. Stern, and Toni S. Gould, *Experimenting with Numbers: Structural Arithmetic for Kindergarten* (Boston: Houghton Mifflin, 1966).

21. John C. Gray, *Number by Development: A Method of Number Instruction* (Philadelphia: Lippincott, 1910). I hope that someone will eventually transcribe Gray's arithmetic method for the computer. There are programs of this type under development—see, for example, W. Feurzeig and B. Y. White, *An Articulate Instructional System for Teaching*

Arithmetic Procedures (Cambridge, Mass.: Bolt, Beranek and Newman, n.d.)—but none to my knowledge is as extensive and detailed as Gray's.

22. James McLellan and John Dewey, *The Psychology of Number* (New York: Appleton, 1895).
23. Ibid., p. 26.
24. Charles C. Fries, *Linguistics and Reading* (New York: Holt, Rinehart and Winston, 1962); Resnick and Ford, *The Psychology of Mathematics for Instruction.*

7 / MAKING THE BEST OF THINGS

1. George A. Miller and P. M. Gildea, "How Children Learn Words," *Scientific American* 257 (1987): 94–99.
2. J. R. Levin, "The Mnemonic '80s: Keywords in the Classroom," *Educational Psychologist* 16 (1981): 65–82.
3. Albert Shanker, president of the American Federation of Teachers, makes this point succinctly in one of his editorials, "The Myth of 'Real Schools' . . . And the Reality of Failure," *New York Times* April 9, 1989, sect. E, p. 7. The following books, in discussing the difficulties involved in changing school systems, provide a picture of the extreme degree to which personnel and policies are dedicated to keeping schools the way they are: Roald Campbell, Luvern Cunningham, Raphael Nystrand, and Michael Usdan, *The Organization and Control of American Schools* (Columbus, Ohio: Merrill, 1980); John Goodlad, *A Place Called School: Prospects for the Future* (New York: McGraw-Hill, 1984); Gene Hall and Shirley Hord, *Change in Schools: Facilitating the Process* (Albany: State University of New York Press, 1987); *Aspects of Educational Change* (New York: Wiley, 1976).
4. Christopher Hurn, *The Limits and Possibilities of Schooling* (Boston: Allyn and Bacon, 1978); Daniel Levine and Robert Havighurst, *Society and Education* (Boston: Allyn and Bacon, 1989).
5. Lee Canter, "You Can Do It: Discipline," *Instructor*, September 1979.

6. Ibid., p. 110.
7. Rudolf Dreikurs and Pearl Cassel, *Discipline without Tears* (New York: Hawthorn, 1972).
8. Ibid., pp. 32–33.
9. Ibid., pp. 34–39.
10. Ibid., p. 81.
11. For a review of the history of the evaluation movement in education, and its relationship to politics and policies, see Blaine Worthen and James Sanders, *Educational Evaluation: Alternative Approaches and Practical Guidelines* (New York: Longman, 1987), chap. 2.
12. Daniel Berliner, "In Pursuit of the Expert Pedagogue," *Educational Researcher* 15 (August/September 1986): 5–13.
13. Bruce Tuckman, *Evaluating Instructional Programs* (Boston: Allyn and Bacon, 1985). This book, with Worthen and Sanders, *Educational Evaluation*, provides a balanced overview of contemporary evaluation methods and philosophy, as practiced by the educational profession. On the more controversial aspects of the testing movement, see Edward B. Fiske, "America's Test Mania," and related articles published in a special issue of the *New York Times: Education Life*, April 10, 1988.
14. Ann L. Brown and Annemarie Palinscar, "Reciprocal Teaching of Comprehension Strategies: A Natural History of One Program for Enhancing Learning," in *Intelligence and Cognition in Special Children: Comparative Studies of Giftedness, Mental Retardation, and Learning Disabilities,* ed. J. B. Borkowski and J. D. Day (Norwood, N.J.: Ablex, 1988).
15. Arnold Gesell, *The Mental Growth of the Preschool Child* (New York: Macmillan, 1926); Arnold Gesell, Frances Ilg, and Louise Ames, *The Child from Five to Ten* (New York: Harper and Row, 1977). These are only two of the many books from the Yale clinic. They have gone in and out of fashion, in part because of new pediatric publications and in part because of paradigmatic shifts in the study of child development—away from observation and toward experimental manipulation. The Gesell materials are of classic

scientific importance, however, and remain, in my judgment, superb guides to child rearing.

16. Louise Bates Ames, *Is Your Child in the Wrong Grade?* (New York: Harper and Row, 1967), p. 1. An earlier publication was Frances Ilg and Louise Bates Ames, *School Readiness* (New York: Harper and Row, 1965).

17. Ames, *Is Your Child in the Wrong Grade?* p. 56.

18. An attempt to determine the best age for learning standardized materials, such as addition facts and double-digit multiplication, was made by C. W. Washburne and his colleagues in the 1920s. They conducted an experiment that would now be difficult to manage, but whose results were quite informative. Children across a five-year age spread were all taught the same materials in the same way. Their rate of learning was closely monitored. It is possible to determine from these learning curves, for example, that ten-year-olds can learn something in a week that it would take eight-year-olds two months to learn. In general, the research suggested that attempting to teach children standardized materials at earlier and earlier ages is highly inefficient. See C. W. Washburne, "The Grade Placement of Arithmetic Topics," in *The 29th Yearbook of the National Society for the Study of Education*, ed. B. R. Brownell (Bloomington: Public School Publishing Co., 1930); C. W. Washburne, "The Work of 'The Committee of Seven' on Grade-Placement in Arithmetic," in *Child Development and the Curriculum: The 38th Yearbook of the National Society for the Study of Education*, ed. G. M. Whipple (Bloomington: Public School Publishing Co., 1939).

8 / MAKING THINGS BETTER

1. See Chapter 7, note 3, and "The 13th Annual Gallup Poll of the Public's Attitudes toward the Public Schools," as reported by George Gallup in *Phi Delta Kappan* (September 1981): 33–47. See also Diane Ravitch, *Schools We De-*

serve: Reflections on the Educational Crisis of Our Time (New York: Basic, 1985).

2. Edward B. Fiske, "High Schools Are His Laboratories," *New York Times* Education Supplement, November 2, 1986, provides a good introduction to Theodore Sizer's work. In addition, his project has generated three books: Theodore Sizer, *Horace's Compromise: The Dilemma of the American High School* (Boston: Houghton Mifflin, 1984); Arthur Powell, Eleanor Farrar, and David Cohen, *The Shopping Mall High School: Winners and Losers in the Educational Marketplace* (Boston: Houghton Mifflin, 1985); and Robert Hampel, *The Last Little Citadel* (Boston: Houghton Mifflin, 1985).

3. Memorandum from Dean Frank Murray, College of Education, University of Delaware, 1988.

4. Betsey Brill Granda, "The Beginnings of a School: A Personal Perspective" (Master's thesis, Bank Street College of Education, 1978); the school is also described in a newspaper report, written by Charles Bohner, in the Wilmington, Delaware, *Morning News*, March 26, 1981, p. A19.

5. Among the many publications that are relevant to starting a school: Nickolaus Engelhardt, *Complete Guide for Planning New Schools* (West Nyack, N.Y.: Parker Publishing Co., 1970); A. E. Hardie, "Plenty of Alternatives," *New York Times* Fall Education Survey, November 10, 1986, pp. 42–43; Fred Hechinger, "Better Schools: Issues of Power," *New York Times*, September 23, 1986; Jonathan Kozol, *Alternative Schools: A Guide for Educators and Parents* (New York: Continuum, 1982); William Kraus, *Collaboration in Organizations: Alternatives to Hierarchy* (New York: Human Sciences Press, 1980); Robert Love, *How to Start Your Own School: A Guide for the Radical Right, the Radical Left, and Everybody In-Between Who's Fed Up with Public Education* (New York: Macmillan, 1973); Myron Lieberman, *Beyond Public Education* (New York: Praeger, 1986); and Phillip Sleleman and D. M. Rockwell, *Designing Learning Environments* (New York: Longman, 1981).

6. Patricia Lines, "An Overview of Home Instruction," *Phi Delta Kappan* 68 (1987):510.
7. J. A. Van Galen, "Explaining Home Education: Parents' Accounts of Their Decisions to Teach Their Own Children," *Urban Review* 19 (1987):166.
8. Ibid.
9. Ibid., p. 167.
10. John Holt, *Teach Your Own* (New York: Delacorte Press, 1981), pp. 261–262.
11. Van Galen, "Explaining Home Education," p. 174.
12. Ibid., p. 173.
13. See Holt, *Teach Your Own;* Kay Kuzma, *Teaching Your Own Preschool Children* (Garden City: Doubleday, 1980); Maire Mullarney, *Anything School Can Do You Can Do Better* (Dublin: Arlen House, 1983); Mary Pride, *The New Big Book of Home Learning* (Westchester, Ill.: Crossway, 1988); Van Galen, "Explaining Home Education"; T. E. Wade, *The Home School Manual* (Auburn, Calif.: Gazelle Publications, 1984); Nancy Wallace, *Better Than School: One Family's Declaration of Independence* (Burdett, N.Y.: Larson Publications, 1983).
14. Lines, "An Overview of Home Instruction."

CONCLUSION

1. I am indebted to my colleague David Johns for pointing this out to me. The program was an ABC News presentation called "The Electronic Time Machine," May 18, 1989. For a transcript, write Journal Graphics, 267 Broadway, New York, N.Y. 10007. For a copy of the video, write ABC Distribution Company, 825 Seventh Avenue, New York, N.Y. 10007.
2. For recent coverage of past and present policies, see *Social Goals and Educational Reform* ed. Charles V. Willie and Inabeth Miller (New York: Greenwood Press, 1988). For a book addressing the problems of making predictions, and illustrating how contradictory they can be, see *Future*

Trends in Education Policy, ed. Jane Newitt (Lexington, Mass.: Heath, 1979).
3. Marvin J. Cetron, with Barbara Soriano and Margaret Gayle, *Schools of the Future: How American Business and Education Can Cooperate to Save Our Schools* (New York: McGraw-Hill, 1985).
4. See almost any issue of *Education Week,* published by Editorial Projects in Education, 1255 23rd Street NW, Suite 775, Washington, D.C. 20037. "A Win-Win Situation: School Classrooms in the Workplace," written by Reagan Walker, (*Education Week* 6, no. 39, 1987), for example, describes new school-business partnerships in Dade County, Florida. Seminal books include David Kearns and Denis Doyle, *Winning the Brain Race: A Bold Plan to Make Our Schools Competitive* (San Francisco: Institute for Contemporary Studies Press, 1988), which may be ordered from the Institute at 243 Kearny Street, San Francisco, Calif. 94108; and Jack E. Bowsher, *Educating America: Lessons Learned in the Nation's Corporations* (New York: Wiley, 1989). Kearns is chairman and chief executive officer of Xerox Corporation. Bowsher has recently retired from the job of coordinating employee education at IBM. There is powerful rhetoric in books of this type. Bowsher, for example, describes the hypothetical reaction of an executive in charge of a large organization that manufactures computers, who has discovered grievous problems. Thirty percent of the computers have not made it off the production line; another 20 percent are labeled failures—not usable—and will have to be warehoused, at substantial cost, for forty years; the second quartile are acceptable, but not great; only the top quartile is something to be proud of. If you were this executive, Bowsher says, "Your immediate reaction would undoubtedly be to take a look at the process of manufacturing. You would never suggest running daily production a few hours longer or paying the managers and workers more money with the hope they might make better computers. You would not waste time discussing merit pay . . . Your entire focus would be on the *process*. Likewise, it

is time to study the *process of education* before billions more dollars are added to the cost of education. This book represents an attempt to motivate the leaders of government, business, and education to shift their time, knowledge, creativity, and resources away from defining the problems toward finding breakthrough solutions" (pp. 7–8).

Suggested Reading

HISTORY AND PROBLEMS OF TODAY'S SCHOOLS

Lawrence A. Cremin, *The Transformation of the School* (New York: Random House, 1964).

Albert Shanker, "Where We Stand," weekly columns in News of the Week in Review, *New York Times.*

Charles Silberman, *Crisis in the Classroom* (New York: Random House, 1970).

COGNITIVE AND DEVELOPMENTAL SCIENCE

Bernard Baars, *The Cognitive Revolution in Psychology* (New York: Guilford, 1986).

Jerome Bruner, *In Search of Mind: Essays in Autobiography* (New York: Harper and Row, 1983).

Dorothy Cohen, *The Learning Child: Guidelines for Parents and Teachers* (New York: Random House, 1973).

THE BASICS

Robert C. Aukerman, *Approaches to Beginning Reading* (New York: John Wiley, 1984).

Herbert Ginsburg, *Children's Arithmetic: How They Learn It and How You Teach It* (Austin, Tex: Pro-Ed, 1989).

Seymour Papert, *Mindstorms: Children, Computers, and Powerful Ideas* (New York: Basic Books, 1980).

William Zinsser, *Writing to Learn* (New York: Harper and Row, 1988).

Credits

Verses from "The Four Georges," in Peter Hancock and Robert Long, *Kings and Things* (London: BBC Radio for Schools, 1979), appear by permission of BBC Schools Radio.

FIGURES

1. Audrey B. Champagne and Joan Rogalska-Saz, "Computer-Based Numeration Instruction," LRDC technical report, Learning Research and Development Center, University of Pittsburgh, fig. 1. Used by permission.
2. Scottish Examination Board, Dalkieth, Scotland. Used by permission.
4 (and Table 3). Used by permission of Deborah C. Smith, Director, Curriculum Development Lab, College of Education, University of Delaware.
6. Barbara Y. White and Paul Horwitz, "ThinkerTools: Enabling Children to Understand Physical Laws," report no. 6470, BBN Laboratories, Bolt, Beranek and Newman, Inc., Cambridge, Massachusetts. Used by permission.
8. Redrawn from Michael Holt and Zoltan Dienes, *Let's Play Math* (New York: Walker and Company, 1973); © 1973 by Michael Holt and Zoltan Dienes. Used by permission of Walker and Company, A. P. Watts, Ltd., and Michael Holt.

10, 11, and 12. John C. Gray, *Number by Development: A Method of Number Instruction* (Philadelphia: Lippincott, 1910), pp. 67, 77, 101.

PHOTOS

p. 8	Barbara Alper (Stock, Boston)
p. 30	Patricia Ann Schwab (Stock, Boston)
p. 54	George W. Gardner (Stock, Boston)
p. 74	Elizabeth Crews (Stock, Boston)
p. 92	Elizabeth Crews (Stock, Boston)
p. 116	Elizabeth Crews (Stock, Boston)
p. 144	Elizabeth Hamlin (Stock, Boston)
p. 168	Bohdan Hrynewych (Stock, Boston)

Index

Achievement tests, 158, 165–166; vs. classroom grading, 160–162

Adler, Alfred, 152

Alternative programs, starting, 169–188, 192–195; working model for, 169, 170–175; within the existing system, 169, 175–179, 217n3; starting a new school, 170, 179–181, 185–186, 220n5; home schooling, 170, 181–185; dissemination plan, 170, 175; apprenticeship for prospective teachers, 170, 174–175; curriculum packages, 170, 175, 177; collecting information, 170–172, 178–179; working group for, 172, 175, 180–181; decision making, 175–187; risks and rewards in, 187–188

Alternative school, starting, 170, 179–181, 185–186, 220n5; requirements for, 170–175. *See also* Alternative programs, starting

Ames, Louise Bates, 163–165

Apprenticeship, cognitive, 5, 159–160, 190

Apprenticeship model, 55–73, 118, 128–129, 169, 172–174, 192–193; principles of, 56–73; complex, situated learning in, 56–57; expert models in, 58–60; mind of student as curriculum, 60–63; learning as a social enterprise, 63–66; role of teacher in, 66–70; teaching methods in, 67–70, 71; multicultural perspective in, 70–73; computers and, 104–114; programs, 194–195

Architecture of cognition, 34 (fig.), 34–41, 56; pick-up system, 35, 41–42; buffers, 35; and behavioral output, 35; and goals, 36–37; working memory, 35–37, 42–44; long-term memory, 37–38, 44–48

Aristotle, 37

Arithmetic, 131–141, 216n21; problem-solving strategies, 131–134; computation and calculation in, 134; first-order skills in, 134; counting and addition, 136–138; multiplication, 138; simple equations, 138; subtraction, 138–141; division, 141. *See also* Mathematics

Articulation, as teaching method, 69

Artificial intelligence, 31, 37, 203n3

Arts, 69; and aesthetic scaffolding, 76, 80–81; in social studies curriculum, 76–77, 80–81, 84, 85, 90

229